Spurred by Grace
Bound by Love

Spurring one another on.....

Thirty-five years of
friendship and faith

Compiled by
Kathleen Page Clark
Clarice Townes Miller

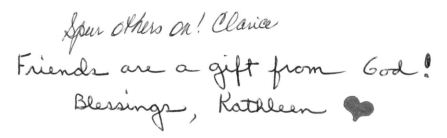

Spur others on! Clarice

Friends are a gift from God!
Blessings, Kathleen

xulon PRESS

Spurred by Grace
Bound by Love
Thirty-five years of friendship and faith

Table of Contents

Introduction   Why did we feel called to write this book?
Preface   Meet the Spurs
Contributors and Hometowns
Dedication
Acknowledgments
Endorsement

Introduction:
Why did we feel called to write this book?
by Clarice Townes Miller

The body is a unit, though it is made up of many parts;
and though all its parts are many,
they form one body. So it is with Christ.
I Corinthians 12:12

For those with any writing experience, it is well known how important it is to have a clear understanding as to the purpose of a book.

Finding a unified, concise statement was as varied as each contributor to this Spurs' collection of stories.

Here are some of the reasons for this book:

- Our children, grandchildren and great-grandchildren need to know these stories. That is why we initially started this book. We think these stories will show a depth and humor of their mother, grandmother, great-grandmother, etc. that they might never hear otherwise.
- We want it to be seen how we have been and continue to be glory reflectors of God's faithfulness, blessings and goodness through the years.
- It might encourage other women to start a group like ours.
- This might answer the question we are most often asked: "How does a group of women stay together for over thirty-five years?"

- Perhaps someone out there who is fed up with "women's groups" might see a fresh benefit of a group like this one.
- Many of us have been asked by others to publish our stories in a book.
- This collection of our stories is proof of God's faithfulness, that prayer works, joy comes in the morning and His Word is Truth.
- People need to know how much fun a group of Christian women can have together.
- We are living proof that a group of Christian women are not exempt from any of life's experiences. We are witnesses to the fact that a group like the Spurs helps us get through the tough times. We are there to celebrate together when we get to the other side of pain. We are also there to celebrate our many joys!
- For those who have lost the joy of being a Christian, please read on!

Our prayer and dream is that as you read this book, you will find that many of these reasons have made your read worthwhile.

Blessings.

Preface: Meet the Spurs

by Clarice Townes Miller and Kathleen Page Clark

*And let us consider how we may **spur** one another on
toward love and good deeds.
Let us not give up meeting together, as some are
in the habit of doing,
but let us encourage one another—
and all the more as you see the Day approaching.
Hebrews 10:24-25 (NIV 1984)*

*Y*ou, the reader, are about to begin an unbelievable adventure as you meet the Spurs, a group of committed Christian ladies who have been meeting together for over thirty-five years. You can see from the above Scripture how we got our name. We are **not** rodeo queens or a sports team! We feel it is important for you to know a few things about us that make this group of women unique.

1. We live in different cities.
2. We grew up in different parts of the United States.
3. We are different ages.
4. We are different sizes.
5. We are made up of married, widowed, and divorced women.
6. We are from a wide range of economic status.
7. We are all Christians.
8. The Spurs collectively come from a background of ten different denominations:

- Assembly of God
- Baptist
- Bible Church
- Catholic
- Episcopalian
- Lutheran
- Methodist
- Non-Denominational
- Presbyterian
- The Vineyard

As Ecclesiastes 3:1-8 says:

There is a time for everything, and a season for every activity under heaven: a time to be born and a time to die, a time to plant and a time to uproot, a time to kill and a time to heal, a time to tear down and a time to build, a time to weep and a time to laugh, a time to mourn and a time to dance, a time to scatter stones and a time to gather them, a time to embrace and a time to refrain, a time to search and a time to give up, a time to keep and a time to throw away, a time to tear and a time to mend, a time to be silent and a time to speak, a time to love and a time to hate, a time for war and a time for peace.

This particular Scripture gave us the framework, ideas and some titles for our stories. The Spurs, do indeed, have a story for each of these scriptures, but there is no way that we could include all of our stories. Some are too personal, private, painful or embarrassing! You will realize, though, that we have experienced life from the greatest joys to the deepest sorrows together.

We can think of no life events that the Spurs have not experienced. Many are writing their stories for the first time. This has been a healing and a blessing. We hope your read will be a healing and a blessing for you as well.

Some helpful comments, as you start to read. If in the story a person's first name is used, you will know she is a Spur. We did have two Carolyns at one time however, so we use their last names for clarification. The list of names and hometowns are included here. There is a short bio and photo of each Spur at the end of the book.

So get ready to share some of our collective journeys! Get ready to laugh, cry and be amazed. We pray you will benefit from our experiences and that you will see how faithful God is in all circumstances. We hope to encourage you in whatever situation you find yourself. We pray you are blessed by reading this book. God bless you.

Left to right: Clarice Townes Miller and Kathleen Page Clark.

Contributors and Hometowns

Just as our bodies have many parts
and each part has a special function,
so it is with Christ's body.
We are many parts of one body,
and we all belong to each other.
Romans 12:4-5 (NLT)

Spurs
Hometown

Carolyn Bergstrom Boyd	Weatherford, Texas
Mary Alice Cowen Brumley	Fort Worth, Texas
Elizabeth Davis Buckley	Lexington, Kentucky
Kathleen Page (Elliott) Clark	Horseshoe Bay, Texas
Barbara Clarkin	Fort Worth, Texas
Molly Dummit	Fort Worth, Texas
Lois Maureen Kelsey Eagan	Rockwall, Texas
Anne Johnson Hyde	Fort Worth, Texas
Mimi Taylor Mack	Fort Worth, Texas
Clarice Townes Miller	Nacogdoches, Texas
Gayle Scott O'Neal	Weatherford, Texas
Sally Tull Renshaw	Decatur, Texas
Pat Geis Reynolds	Dallas, Texas
Sandra Adams Talkington	Arlington, Texas
Harriet Jane Wallace	Dallas, Texas
Phyllis Webster White	Fort Worth, Texas
Carol Kinney Williams	Dallas, Texas

Deceased

Carolyn Driggers Mallone	Arlington, Texas
Suzie Martin Murray	Fort Worth, Texas
Mary Jo Scheideman	Fort Worth, Texas
Janet Sheats	Fort Worth, Texas
Georgia Smith	Brock, Texas

Moved away

Virginia Kahler	Santa Fe, New Mexico

Honorary Spur

Mary Guenzel	Colorado Springs, Colorado

A Spur event, December 2004.

Left to right standing: Carolyn Boyd, Mary Alice Brumley, Anne Hyde, Harriet Wallace, Pat Reynolds, Sally Renshaw, Phyllis White, Maureen Eagan, Georgia Smith, Kathleen Page Clark.

Left to right seated: Mary Jo Scheideman, Molly Dummit, Sandra Talkington, Gayle O'Neal, Clarice Townes Miller, Mimi Mack

Dedication

I thank God, whom I serve, as my ancestors did,
with a clear conscience, as night and day
I constantly remember you in my prayers.
Recalling your tears, I long to see you,
so that I may be filled with joy.
I am reminded of your sincere faith, which first lived
in your grandmother Lois and in your mother Eunice
and, I am persuaded, now lives in you also.
2 Timothy 1:3-5

The Spurs dedicate this book to the children, grandchildren, great-grandchildren and all future generations of the Spurs. As of March 2013, the Spurs have eighty-one children, one hundred eighty-four grandchildren and forty-five great-grand-children. This book was written to encourage them in their faith and to be witnesses to the faithfulness of our Lord and Savior, Jesus Christ.

If the Lord uses this book in any other way to encourage His people, to God be the glory!

Acknowledgments

by Kathleen Page Clark and Clarice Townes Miller

Be joyful always; pray continually;
give thanks in all circumstances,
for this is God's will for you in Christ Jesus.
I Thessalonians 5:16-18

*I*t is evident that God has had, and continues to have, His hand on the life of the Spurs, individually and collectively. He brought us together and by His grace and mercy has sustained this group of women for thirty-five years and counting. During these years, the Spurs shared many life events that have never been publicly told or written. We became more and more convinced that these stories had value if shared and might bring insight, healing, wisdom and encouragement to others. Each Spur has contributed at least one story for the book. It took courage for some of the Spurs to write their stories for publication. Some are still locked in the hearts of the Spurs, and placed in the gentle hands of a loving God. We thank the Spurs for their trust and blessing for the two of us to prepare the book for publication. We are grateful to God for the life of each Spur and her part in contributing to this book.

A book takes on a life of its own, from being a dream to becoming a reality. There were moments of spurts and stalls over the years. Then, just like God does in His perfect timing, He sent people into our lives to spur the dream into a reality. We are especially grateful for the contributions of six friends He sent to us:

Kerry Moynagh: Kerry attended our 2011 Christmas gathering at the Scheideman home. She works for a New York publisher and is a wonderful photographer. She gave us some professional guidelines and took candid and individual photos of us for the book. Thank you, God, for Kerry's willingness to come to Texas to share her expertise and gifts with us.

Helen Kooiman Hosier: Helen came into the life of the Spurs and our book project at the perfect time. Helen is a renowned author, biographer, compiler and editor of many Christian books. She asked to see the manuscript and she edited the book twice for us. Our new friend gave us encouragement and wise professional advice. She spurred us on by telling us that there is not a book "out there" like our book and to "press on." She encouraged us to publish it. Helen also wrote the book endorsement. Thank you, God, for the providential timing of Helen's friendship.

Tom Clark: This book may not have ever gone to print without the help of Tom Clark. He married Kathleen Page Elliott on May 27, 2012. Tom was God's gift to Kathleen but he was also a gift to the Spurs. At that time, the Spur book was at a standstill. We weren't sure where to turn next. Little did we know that God was not only giving Kathleen a loving husband, but Tom was giving the Spurs the nudge that we needed to finish our book. Tom spurred us on with great patience and expertise. His editing skills were invaluable. He did hours of research to find the best self-publisher for this book. He had the computer skills needed to prepare the text and photos for submitting the manuscript to the publisher. Tom has gotten to know the Spurs quickly by name and face while working with the stories and photos. He feels blessed to have been a part of the process. He sees it as a ministry because he knows that God will use this book in ways we can only imagine. God gets all the credit. If you were to ask Tom what this experience has been like, we think he would respond: "The Spur book project has proven that Kathleen and I are a great team. We are very compatible and complement each other. The book has consumed seven of the first nine months of our marriage. We look forward to life after the book."

Jon Holiday: Discovering Jon and his beautiful photography is another example of God's perfect timing. Jon graciously gave us permission to use his copyrighted photo entitled "Springtime Sunset in Texas" for the cover of this book. Jon is a prolific photographer who has won many awards in international venues. Especially known for his city skylines, Jon's current focus is TexasScapes, which includes natural settings with bluebonnets and wildflowers. Most of his body of work is made up of "Beautiful Places" subjects, and has been frequently used in office, restaurant, and healthcare environments. He loves taking pictures in and around his hometown of Fort Worth, Texas, where he and his wife of twenty-seven years and his twenty-year-old daughter are active in church and community. Explore all of Jon's "beautiful" work at www.photosbyjon.com.

Kristin Page-Elliott Kirkland: A special thanks to Kristin, who not only did the "right" thing by submitting a wonderful story and photo for our book, but was also extremely helpful in suggesting cover designs and layouts. Thank you, Kristin, for sharing your gifts and talents with the Spurs.

Patricia (Patty) Goetsch Hundley: The first edition of the book was a pre-Patty Hundley read. We are grateful for the time and talent she gave this edition with her fresh eyes and a love for grammar! Thank you, Patty!

We thank the many contributors to this book: Spurs, husbands, children and grandchildren. It took each one to make it possible for you to actually hold this book in your hands.

Dreams do come true! Thank you, God, for simple dreams that become a reality. We pray for the life this book now takes on.

Endorsement

You hold in your hands an amazing book—a collaborative effort by a dedicated group of women committed to each other, uncompromising in their faith and devotion to God. Even at our best, fallible creatures that we are, to succeed at staying together for thirty-five years and counting is truly amazing. However, there is something more—one senses the sure hand of God upon the lives of these friends, as He has providentially drawn and held them together. I remember these lines, familiar words I love:

God's Handwriting
He writes in characters too grand
for our short sight to understand;
we watch but broken strokes, and try
to fathom all the mystery
of withered hopes, of death, of life,
the endless war, the useless strife –
but there, with larger, clearer sight
we shall see this—His way was right.
John Oxenham from *Bees in Amber*

I come back to my first statement—this is truly an amazing book. You will be inspired, motivated and blessed, held in the grip of God's love, as you read.

Helen Kooiman Hosier
Author, Biographer, Compiler, Editor

Spurred by Grace
Chapter One

A Time for Memories

A Time to Begin
Beginnings
by Carolyn Boyd

*And let us consider how we may spur one another on
toward love and good deeds.*
Hebrews 10:24

The year 1977 had been a very hard year for us. On January 30, our home was completely destroyed by fire and our family was devastated. We only had lived in our dream home fourteen months when I planned a big birthday celebration for my husband's fortieth birthday. The tables were set, the food prepared and only the final touches had to be added the next day.

Jim was at Harris Hospital on one of those middle-of-the-night calls, delivering a baby, which would probably keep him at the hospital for the rest of the night. I went to bed exhausted. The children were at various places—Keith at the church for a lock-in, Karan spending the night with a girlfriend, and Debbie was the only one home with me.

At 5:00 a.m. I awakened to a flickering light coming into the bedroom. I got up to investigate why a lamp would be flickering in the early morning hours. To my horror, I saw the back portion of the house ablaze with flames leaping onto our shingle-roofed house and causing a severe threat to the neighborhood. Finding our phone dead, I grabbed our five-year-old and rushed to our neighbor's house for help.

The rest is history—everything was destroyed and within hours we were homeless; we had no clothes to put on our backs, nor a place to take refuge. We had lots of work ahead of us to put our lives back together. We accepted the challenge and within ten months had rebuilt the house and had begun all over again.

When my friend Pat, a social worker in Dallas, called me late in October of 1977 to check on how we were doing, I admitted I was spiritually depleted and very weary. I asked her what she was doing at that particular time and she said she had been conducting weekend retreats for women using Phillip Keller's book, *A Shepherd Looks at the Twenty-third Psalm.* That interested me and I asked her if she would do a weekend for me if I would gather some of my friends together. We looked at the calendar and set a date for later that year. We would meet at our lake house in Granbury, Texas.

I checked with some of my friends and they were very interested in doing something like that. Pat brought along some people from Dallas as well. We gathered for what we thought would be a good weekend of teaching and fun and then we would return to our lives refreshed and inspired. However, what was intended to be a weekend of sharing and praying for one another, became a group that has bonded and one that has held each other through many hard places. We have prayed together, traveled together, supported one another and have loved each other like sisters. We are from many denominations, diverse backgrounds, varied lifestyles and many personality types; yet, bonded beyond belief!

As our group continued to meet, we took Hebrews 10:23-25 (NIV 1984) to heart.

Let us hold unswervingly to the hope we profess, for he who promised is faithful. And let us consider how we may spur one another on toward love and good deeds. Let us not give up meeting together, as some are in the habit of doing, but let us encourage one another—and all the more as you see the Day approaching.

That was over thirty-five years ago. We truly have become sisters in Christ. This is a story of God's unconditional love—we are merely working "out" what He has worked "in" us. We love each other because He has showered love on us.

One of the original Spurs, Carolyn Boyd *(left)*, and one of the newest Spurs, Harriet Wallace *(right)*.

A Time for Reflection
Spurred on by Love
by Clarice Townes Miller

To them God has chosen to make known among the Gentiles
the glorious riches of this mystery,
which is Christ in you, the hope of glory.
Colossians 1:27

*H*ow does one describe a shooting star or the mystery of the birth of a baby? How does an artist capture a sunset over the ocean on canvas?

As I think of the mystery of the Spurs, I am at a loss for the descriptive words that describe who we are! God has brought together ladies with varied personalities, interests, religious denominations and goals in life. He has woven our lives together through these thirty-five plus years so beautifully that we are a tapestry of His divine grace! When others ask who we are and how we started, it's equally impossible to explain. Some knew each other through our husbands working together; some were friends in their various cities and churches. We came and found something within this particular group of friends that none of us have with any other. It's a gift of God to each of us that we have embraced and enjoyed through these many years. That doesn't mean we haven't had our moments of uneasiness, questioning and having to work through differences. Amazingly, we have stayed together all these years.

We gather to share our lives, joys, struggles and insights. We pray for one another and ask for and receive blessings from God and each other. We share a meal and hurry back to our individual lives.

In the beginning we met monthly or whenever one had an urgent need or crisis. It is astounding to each of us the variety of needs we had and have. If one would look at us as a group or individually, most would not believe the pain that we have shared. We would be labeled as a group of enviable, socially prominent and active, upper middle-class women who have few problems or needs.

The secret of why we have lasted so long and God has blessed our group is because we have been so willing to be open, honest, vulnerable with and accountable to one another. Through seeking God's will and the group's support, we receive healing, comfort and wisdom in facing our challenges.

Not only do we pray individually, we pray collectively and know that we will continue to support each other this way.

As we pool our life experiences, we walk through the rawness of life together. Through God's grace and the love of each other, we have been comforted in our moments of pain. Our stories include alcoholism, drug addictions, unfaithful husbands, divorce, depression, rape of a mother, death of children and grandchildren, murder of a child and death of five of our beloved Spurs.

Our love for one another and our faith in God has grown tremendously. We have experienced the Kingdom of God here on earth. Something of the Divine beyond our describing takes place that we recognize as holy. We sense His Presence in our midst. Our families sense a difference in us when we come home.

We come with our diversity. Our love of one another and the oneness of God overpower our differences. We experience that "peace that passes all understanding" when we come in our brokenness with our multiple problems and heartaches. We pour ourselves out to Him and to each other. We leave filled with His Spirit.

When we started meeting years ago we were in our twenties, thirties and forties; now we are in our sixties, seventies and eighties. What important lessons have we learned?

1. God is with us reconciling us back to Himself. He uses daily life events to get our attention. Others reflect what God wants us to see.
2. It is through telling our stories that we are healed, loved and comforted. Telling our stories gives each of us encouragement and courage to live out our lives.
3. Unfolding trust and safety have been built through the years.
4. God uses our differences to help us stretch and mature.
5. Ministering to one another connects our families.
6. Our discovery of each other is still continuing.
7. God has richly interwoven our lives together so that many of our children and grandchildren know and love each other.
8. Our husbands have been blessed by our growth. We are more relaxed, energized, and calmer for having shared with God and each other whatever has been on our hearts. They "reap the benefit" when we return home.
9. We gain strength, courage and confidence by every experience when we stop to look fear in the face.
10. Even though some in the group have been together for more than thirty-five years, we are mindful of the importance to continue spurring each other on, especially "all the more as you see the Day approaching."
11. The Spurs had a simple beginning with eternal benefits!
12. In spite of many heartaches we have shared together, we all agree that our signature sound is laughter. We have SO much fun together!

A Time to Reminisce
Continue to Pray
by Molly Dummit

Continue in prayer and watch in the same with thanksgiving.
Colossians 4:2 (KJV)
Devote yourselves to prayer, being watchful and thankful.
Colossians 4:2

*H*ow do you write a short story covering over thirty-five years of caring and sharing?

When the Spurs began in 1977, I was forty-eight-years old and my daughter was twenty-six. We were part of the original group of ladies destined to become the Spurs. For most of that time we were the oldest and youngest and are the only mother-daughter Spurs.

I bonded immediately with the group but had no idea what God had in store for me with these loving, dedicated women. Since I was a child I had stuffed pain and shame all the way down into my toes. This was bursting to be released and God had prepared a cushion for me in the loving arms of these new Christian friends.

I was born in the Deep South and I knew how to deal with pain! Just stick your head in the sand and don't dare to look or feel. That was my motto! Not so with the Spurs—we believed in inner healing and growing stronger in the Lord.

My handsome son, a Navy Medic, had come home from Vietnam, wounded and scarred. My mother was now old and still had a problem with an illness for which I had no understanding. I was heavily burdened but the Spurs patiently helped set me free. God is always available when there is a crisis, a joyous celebration, a sickness or need. So are the Spurs.

The most important times I have spent with the Spurs have been our times of prayer together. We pray for husbands, children, grandchildren, great-grandchildren, family and friends, our country and leaders—anyone in need. We praise God for answered prayer, healing, comfort and protection for each other.

Through the years we have experienced many health issues. Think of any illness that you or another family could experience: diabetes, cancers, heart attacks, surgeries of all kinds, accidents, hip and knee replacements, Alzheimer's dementia, broken bones and broken hearts, lightening burns, AIDS, alcoholism, drugs, assault, rape, kidnapping, multiple sclerosis, Lou Gehrig's disease, Down syndrome—even murder! All of these things have brought us to our knees! It's hard to believe, even for us, that all these things have happened.

There have been many times of celebration, too. We've presented many with a personalized scrapbook telling of our love and what their lives have meant to us. Beautiful memories!

We've celebrated with our daughters at dinners and retreats in their honor. It's been a wonderful way to get to know them, too.

The Spurs are great encouragers at times of joy—weddings, birthdays, graduations, and births. Different gifts and creativity are a big part of the personality of this group. All our leaders are very creative. Some are decorators, gourmet cooks, musicians, singers, artists, writers and saleswomen—all in all, a delightful variety. We are from varied churches, denominations and backgrounds. Church doctrine and different theology perspectives have never been an issue. Each of us has held jobs in our churches as Sunday school teachers, Bible leaders, elders, retreat speakers and prayer partners but that is rarely discussed. We honor Jesus' command to "love one another as I have loved you."

We've built a beautiful trust and loyalty among ourselves. *We who believe are carefully joined together as a constant growing temple for God (Eph. 2:21).* Now, if you think I am telling you our relationships have been or are perfect, I'm not! I know of at least three instances where we hit a "bump in the road" and had to "get out and repair the road" before we could proceed. We have learned to blend, be blended and to bend. We have learned to listen, walk in another's shoes, forgive and offer grace.

If only I, an artist, could paint a picture of the many instances and years of laughter we have shared. On one occasion, we were all together at a retreat in Missouri. It was just before going to bed and we had on our PJ's and robes. Kathleen, a graduate of Stanford, was going back to speak at her thirty-fifth reunion, shortly after our gathering. She had been a Dollie (pom-pom girl) at Stanford. We were delighted when she agreed to perform for us. She did her performance flawlessly! Quite a few others in the group had been cheerleaders in high school. Georgia, our oldest, and Gayle came tripping across the living room, turning high in the air and landing on the floor with one knee up and one knee down—only to be dismayed that they were not able to get up! Laughter turned into hysterical giggles!

Laughter has reverberated over the years in the form of a joke told to me by a surgeon visiting us from Florida. It was so hysterical, I could hardly contain myself. I was bursting to tell my friends. I cornered Mimi and Carolyn in a three-stall restroom on our way to a retreat. I began the joke and was so overcome by laughter and spelling some of the words that I did not want to say aloud, that we became hysterical. We were laughing so hard we could hardly breathe. Finally, we emerged from the restroom to find a long line waiting outside. Through the years, I was repeatedly encouraged to tell the joke over, over and over! I have written out the joke in this book so that I don't have to tell it anymore!

As for service, we have reached out in our communities, working and volunteering. A list of Spurs' services is anonymously listed in a following chapter titled "A Time to Serve." We have missionary children in our own Spur family, one in Thailand and one in Japan. We also have two full-time ordained ministers in the United States. Ten of us were involved in starting a clinic in Ethiopia for AIDS mothers with babies. One of us made a trip to western Africa to visit an orphanage her church supports. Many have been on mission and medical trips around the world. This has been a valuable part of our years together.

During our thirty-five years, Pat has given us words to live by for a particular year. Some have been Serendipity, Faith, Fear Not, Courage, and Grace. Some years we would study certain scriptures for months. Nothing was structured.

Whenever one of the Spurs moved away we had to go as a group to see her surroundings and make sure that all was well. Elizabeth moved to Tyler, Texas—off we went to check out her home on Agape Force Ranch. Next, Kathleen moved to Los Gatos, California. What fun we had on a trip to visit her! A large group of us flew in and were surprised at the airport by the longest white limousine I have ever seen. We giggled happily all the way to her home! While visiting a beautiful redwood forest, we walked together, dwarfed by the trees, softly singing hymns of praise.

Clarice moved from Denton to seventy acres of pine trees in Nacogdoches, Texas. She and her husband built a beautiful home with an attached guesthouse which the Spurs have enjoyed using. Needless to say, we have been there several times. We have wonderful memories of joy, laughter, tears, good food and special times of sharing and prayer.

Kathleen moved from California to Horseshoe Bay, Texas. We were soon off to christen her home. Elizabeth moved to Lexington, Kentucky. We visited the horse farms and sang in a small church built in the 1800s. One of our favorite memories is singing in different places here and abroad.

Other memorable trips have been to Eagle-Vail and Beaver Creek, Colorado; Park City, Utah; England and Tuscany, Italy. We have been extremely blessed to share so many trips together.

This has been a glimpse of who we are and how God has used us through the years. These years have flown by and so we continue to pray with watchfulness and thanksgiving for each other and our loving Heavenly Father!

Spurred by Grace
Chapter Two

A Time for Laughter

A Time to Hug   by Kathleen Page Clark
A Time to Laugh   by Sandra Talkington
A Time to Tell a Joke   by Molly Dummit
A Time to Shop   by Kathleen Page Clark
A Time to Wake Up   by Gayle O'Neal
A Time to Practice   by Kathleen Page Clark
A Time for Getting to Know You   by Pat Reynolds

A Time to Hug
Hug Attacks
by Kathleen Page Clark

And he has given us this command:
Whoever loves God must also love his brother.
1 John 4:21
We are to greet each other with a Holy hug!
(modified from multiple scriptures)

My dear friend, Sandra, asked me to join the Spurs in the early '80s. Back then, we met for most of the day nearly every month. Each person brought a salad or dessert and we spent from about 10:00 a.m. to 3:00 p.m. together. We were not a study group. We spent the time sharing and praying. We always ran out of time!

I had been with the group for a couple of years before going on a retreat with them to Beaver Creek, Colorado. We all piled into a condo that was co-owned by two of the Spurs. What a wonderful time we had! There were two memorable things that happened that week back in the mid '80s: One that I learned from them and one that I taught to them.

1) The first lesson that I learned from an overnight with the Spurs was that all the other ladies had much prettier nightgowns than I did! Some had matching negligee sets that looked like something someone would wear on their honeymoon! My flannel nightgown looked rather dumpy

next to theirs so I told them I was committed to upgrading my sleepwear when I returned home.

Little did I know that at our farewell luncheon on the way to the Denver airport, the group would present me with a birthday gift. You guessed it! A sexy, hot pink teddy! I was so pleased and proud of it! Since tables nearby were interested in what all the laughter was about, I embarrassed the Spurs by showing it off like a "walk around as you eat fashion show"—by holding it up—not wearing it! We still laugh about it and I still have it, even though it doesn't fit me anymore!

A picture is worth a thousand words!

Kathleen models her hot pink teddy
that was a gift from all the Spurs.
September 1984.

2) The first lesson that I taught the Spurs was how to give "hug attacks." To my disbelief, they had never heard of one much less given one.

One day while out shopping in a nearby Colorado town, I noticed a man on the other side of the street that needed a hug attack. I gave them a quick refresher and I told them on the count of three that we would go run over and give the man a group hug.

As you might expect, out of the group of about twelve of us, I think only one or two actually went with me! Needless to say, the man was pleasantly surprised and loved it!

About five years later, the Spurs traveled to England together. At the London airport, I gave the Spurs a second chance for a group hug attack. As you can see by this photo, again only two went for the challenge! He loved it!

Kathleen called for a Spur hug attack at the London airport. Carolyn Boyd was the only Spur who joined her.

Prior to the retreat in Colorado, the trip to England and ever since that time, I have continued to give hug attacks. My children and grandchildren get them often. It is a great way to wake someone up! Pile on—but only if it is a reasonable wake-up time or you might be greeted with some unpleasant groans!

It does not take a group of two or more to give hug attacks. I give them one-on-one many times. Being the age we are (now in our 60s, 70s and 80s) we can get away with doing fun and crazy things like this!

Where I live, there are a lot of retired people and a surprising number of Purple Heart license plates. If I see who belongs to the car, I will go up to them and say, "Are you the Purple Heart recipient?" They always say, "Yes" and then I ask them if they have had their "Purple Heart hug" today. Every one of them smiles, says "No" and gladly receives my hug. There are often tears in their eyes when they say, "Thank you." It is never too late to express our gratitude to those who have served our country!

My favorite hug story happened while I was writing this story. Once again, I was at the Post Office and pulled in beside a car with Purple Heart license tags. I caught a glimpse of him from the back so recognized him when he was getting his mail. I asked him the usual question about the "hug for the day" and he eagerly welcomed his. He then told me this heartwarming, encouraging story I love to share.

This man was telling me that for years he never got his Purple Heart license tags. He was modest and did not feel the need to let the world know. Then he learned that there are many perks, like free parking at public places, so he decided to get one. He told me that one week he was a speaker at a Vietnam reunion in New Mexico. He talked about his Purple Heart plates and said that there is one great benefit to having them above all others. He told all of them that "There is a lady in Horseshoe Bay who gives me a hug of gratitude every time she sees me." I was touched that my hugs meant that much to him.

I travel a great deal since I retired from American Airlines with flight benefits. What a heyday I have at airports hugging all those men and women in desert camouflage uniforms heading to or from overseas. I assure them that they are prayed for daily and to express that to the troops. Again, I see grown men and women with tearful eyes, a sense of pride and a grateful heart.

One time as I turned around to proceed to my gate, another man in civilian clothes stopped me and thanked me for doing what I just did. He said, "I feel it but am too timid to express it." Who knows, maybe that man is now bold enough to give hugs!

I learned the gift of hugging in the early '80s from a favorite speaker and author of mine, Bob Benson, at a Gaither Praise Gathering weekend in Indianapolis. Someone once asked him why it is that he gets so many hugs from so many people. He replied that it is easy! He said it is amazing how many people live life with their arms crossed and if you just open up your arms, people will fall into them. I have found that to be true!

It works. I encourage you to try it—or try it more! I don't know a living soul who does not need, benefit from, or want a hug.

Get ready, Spurs! I pray we will have another chance to do a group hug attack soon and I expect more than two to participate at the count of three!

A Time to Laugh

by Sandra Talkington

A merry heart does good, like medicine....
Proverbs 17:22 (NKJV)

An evening the Spurs remember as one of great laughter started with hesitancy. Even though we had become close, few of our husbands knew each other. We wanted them to become acquainted. Our husbands were a little apprehensive about this party.

At the last minute, the plans for the evening were changed. Each Spur was asked to tell one quality about her husband that she appreciated.

I was sitting there thinking about how many times my husband, Ken, had gotten the dishrag out of the garbage disposal for me after I had managed to get it entangled. Then, I thought of how many times he had gotten the sink unstopped when "someone" had put too much grease down the drain. I decided patience was the quality I really appreciated in him.

Each one told of the quality she appreciated in her husband. It was very enlightening, enabled us to get to know everyone's husband better, and turned out to be a fun evening.

When my turn came, I told about how I managed to get the sink stopped up quite often. Each time, Ken would patiently hook up the garden hose, take the outlet cover off, put the hose into the outlet right outside our kitchen window, turn the water on full blast, and, bingo, the water would flow out of the sink like a dream.

The last time I got the sink stopped up, I thought to myself, "I have watched Ken do this over and over. I believe I can do this myself." Also, I hated to ask him one more time. With persistence, I managed to get the outlet cover off. I proceeded to stick the end of the hose into the outlet. When I thought it was in far enough, I turned the water on full blast. It worked! Just like I thought! Only one problem! When I started to pull the hose out, it wouldn't come. I pulled as hard as I could. It wouldn't budge—it was stuck!

I had visions of calling the plumber and trying to explain— maybe having to take bricks out. I showed my share group how I wrapped the hose around my waist and pulled with all my might. That hose would not move an inch. I had no idea that would paint such a funny picture, but they all exploded with laughter.

The story does have a happy ending. I finally confessed to my husband, who was in front of the TV all this time, what I had done. He came out and patiently worked with the hose until he was able to miraculously remove it from the outlet and my sink was in working order again.

I never realized this story would create such laughter, but it is said that laughter is good for the soul! If that is true, our share group should all have very healthy souls because we laugh so much when we are together.

A Time to Tell a Joke
The Suit Joke
by Molly Dummit

*He will yet fill your mouth with laughter
and your lips with shouts of joy.
Job 8:21*

I was always teased, as a child and in adulthood, because of my inability to tell a joke.

A physician was visiting in our home and told the Suit Joke to us just before I left with the Spurs for a retreat at Beaver Creek, Colorado. When he told the Suit Joke we laughed heartily and it was fresh on my mind.

To my deepest regret, I decided to tell it to the Spurs! It is a joke that must be acted out and immediately, when I started to tell it, Maureen began laughing, almost hysterically, and everyone else chimed in. It certainly wasn't THAT funny to me but over the years it became the mascot joke for the Spurs. Whenever we had a slumber party or went on a retreat they coerced me into telling the Suit Joke.

Now, it has been required of me to write it for the book. Oh well, if you can visualize it! Here goes.

The Suit Joke:

A doctor had flown out of town to speak at a meeting. When his luggage did not arrive he had to rush to a haberdashery to purchase a suit. He tried on a gray business suit that fit rather loosely, but since he was in a big hurry, it had to do. There was no time for alterations.

He hurriedly left the store and started down the street. The coat sleeve on his right arm was just too long! He immediately turned around and went back to the clerk exclaiming that something had to be done quickly about that sleeve. The clerk replied, "Oh you can fix that! Just put your chin on your shoulder and pull the sleeve tightly and hold it with your chin." The doctor obeyed and left the store holding his sleeve with his chin. (I am demonstrating to the sounds of loud laughter.)

Down the street a little farther the doctor turned around again and hurried back to the store (all the while with his chin firmly attached to his shoulder). "Look," he exclaimed, "the left leg of these trousers is too long, what can I do?" The clerk was quick to reply. "Just pull your left knee over to your right leg and firmly hold the fabric up by squeezing your knees together." The doctor obeyed again and hobbled out the door—only to return again! He was exasperated by this time and shouted, "Look man, the sleeve of this left arm is too long! I can't go like this." The clerk tried to calm him down and showed him how to pull his left elbow into his left side and hold the sleeve in place.

The doctor started down the street with his right chin on his right shoulder, his knees locked together and his left arm plastered to his side. Two interns were walking toward him as he hobbled down the street. One said to the other, "What would your diagnosis be for that fellow?" The reply came, "I don't know, but did you notice how nice his suit FITS?"

Hysterical laughter from the Spurs every time! Alas, alas, the Spurs have not tired of the Suit Joke but are kind enough not to insist that I tell it anymore. Several years ago, it was put on the shelf.

Molly Dummit tells her famous Suit Joke for the Spurs.

A Time to Shop
(at the Marble Falls Library Thrift Store!)
by Kathleen Page Clark

Keep your lives free from the love of money
and be content with what you have....
Hebrews 13:5

There are two things that you can count on the Spurs doing whenever we travel, wherever we travel, either domestically or internationally:

- We will always find the best restaurants to dine in, so we eat well!
- We will always find the nicest stores to shop in and find a way to fit our purchases in the car or get it boxed to be mailed or go on an airplane!

I have hosted the Spurs on two different occasions at my lakeside home in Horseshoe Bay, Texas.

The first time, the four single Spurs came for the weekend. We had never spent intentional time by ourselves. What fun! Much laughter and relaxation! We have continually talked about doing that again.

The second time, eleven of the Spurs came to my home for a long weekend. My next-door neighbors generously offered the use of their home to accommodate us. We were just a pajama distance away!

I was careful to address the two things that you can count on with the Spurs.

Food: Since I don't cook much (My kitchen just came with the house!), I decided to cater all twelve meals for the four days they were here. A dear friend in my Bible study, Martha Dodd, cooks for church retreats and church dinners, so is talented in cooking for a crowd. She prepared us delicious food for three meals each day (including appetizers and dessert), at a very reasonable cost. We divided up the cost among us. It cost less than eating out and was more pleasant. We could stay in our jammies longer. It was a real treat to only use the kitchen and oven to reheat and serve. Dear Martha Dodd and her husband, Jimmy, made daily deliveries. They enjoyed meeting all my Spur friends whom they had heard about for so many years.

Shopping: I am not a big shopper; however, I do love a good bargain! The closest shopping was six miles away in the town of Marble Falls, Texas.

It is a smart thing to often have no agenda when the Spurs gather because one always surfaces by itself! I made no advance plans while they were here in Horseshoe Bay, but in my heart of hearts, I had a risky hope hidden away. I asked that the Spurs only do one thing while they were here. I asked everyone to get in several cars and follow me to the Marble Falls Library Thrift Store. I told them that everyone had to buy something, even if it were only a ten-cent paperback book.

We did go and invaded the small store. It was one of the most fun hours of the weekend (for me). It was like being on a scavenger hunt. Several were found in the dressing room trying on brand name clothes. Others found treasures to keep or to give away. There was no one empty handed at the checkout counter! I think it might have been the first time some of them had ever been in a thrift store! When we had show-and-tell, our sides were hurting from laughter!

I might add that my purchase, a nicely framed, antique post card of the University of Texas campus, is hanging in Carl

Brumley's insurance office (Carl is the husband of Mary Alice, one of the Spurs). I think I paid two dollars for it! What a treasure!

A picture is worth a thousand words, they say. Here is a photo of us with our bargains standing in front of the store.

The Spurs took the challenge to each find something to buy at the thrift store. What fun!

Left to right: Clarice Townes Miller, Maureen Eagan, Harriet Wallace, Sandra Talkington, Phyllis White, Sally Renshaw, Pat Reynolds, Barbara Clarkin, Mary Alice Brumley, Kathleen Page Clark, Mimi Mack.

A Time to Wake Up

by Gayle O'Neal

"Wake up, O sleeper, rise from the dead,
and Christ will shine on you."
Ephesians 5:14 (NIV 1984)

The Spurs had left on a trip to Beaver Creek, Colorado. My brother had died so I stayed behind to be with my family for our brother's funeral. I was flying into the Denver Airport late at night. Kathleen had offered to come pick me up. When she left the condo, the weather was terrible—it was sleeting and beginning to snow heavily. Many offered to ride to the airport with her, but she said, "No" and off she drove into the blackness of the night.

This was before cell phones, so there was no way for Kathleen and me to let our friends know anything about where we were. About midnight, everyone back at the condo was ready to go to sleep. We arrived at the condo about 2:00 a.m. dead tired! For miles and miles, I had anticipated how good a soft, warm bed would feel. We tiptoed in since all the lights were out and everyone was asleep as we entered.

It is important for you to know that my husband and I owned this condo with several other couples. Just the week before, I had written a check for $800 for our share of the mortgage.

As we crept into the rooms, much to my dismay, I realized that all those warm beds were full of warm bodies. I realized that all the beds had been taken. They had left a blow-up mattress for me to sleep on—but they had not even blown it up! I started going to each bed, jumping in the very middle of those bodies and saying, "Wake Up! Wake Up! Time to get up!"

Within moments we were all awake and laughing hysterically. It has been a memory that we have laughed about for years!

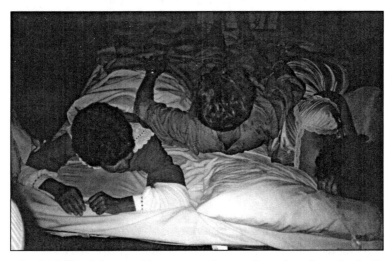

Gayle O'Neal *(center)* jumps on the mother-daughter bed of Elizabeth Buckley *(left)* and Molly Dummit *(right)*.

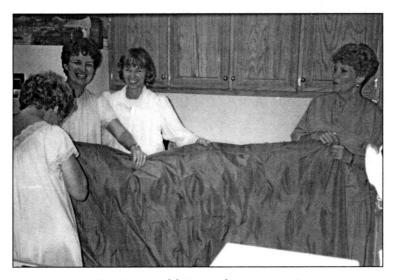

It is time to blow up the mattress!
Left to right: Molly Dummit, Clarice Townes Miller, Sandra Talkington, Gayle O'Neal.

A Time to Practice
Practice pays off
by Kathleen Page Clark

Hold on to instruction, do not let it go;
guard it well, for it is your life.
Proverbs 4:13

It is said, "Practice makes perfect."
It is also said, "Actions speak louder than words."

Here is proof that both statements are true with the Spurs.
Some of the Spurs have *Achy Breaky* down pat!
We are often a silly bunch and laugh until we cry!
There is definitely a lighter side to the Spurs than might be
portrayed in many of our stories.

Photos speak louder than words so judge for yourself.

Left to right: Sally Renshaw, Gayle O'Neal, Molly Dummit and Elizabeth Buckley practice the Achy Breaky in pajamas.

Left to right: Sally Renshaw, Gayle O'Neal, Mary Alice Brumley and Molly Dummit show that practice makes perfect!

A Time for Getting to Know You

by Pat Reynolds

Our mouths were filled with laughter,
our tongues with songs of joy.
Psalm 126:2

Walking inside the mind of an authentic Mississippi southern girl takes insight for pioneer spirited Texans. I had kept my distance from southern women and their Deep South traditions until I met Clarice. We straightforward Texans don't know how to deal with what I perceived as the southern skill of masking critique in sweetness. Clarice came to the Spurs partly for "Southern Belle" recovery. Now, three decades later, I have not seen in Clarice what I had tried to avoid.

The southern way is to keep certain known things hidden by not speaking openly of them. No dark meat in your chicken salad, and even though naked, wear your genuine cultured pearls. They seem to cover a multitude of sins; it may be a proper southern girl's confirmation ritual. Also, please no white shoes after September and get out the dark cotton dresses. Now a good southern girl is ready for fall.

Nevertheless, Deep Southernism is like a kudzu vine; it is never completely vanquished!

I was visiting Hamp and Clarice in early 2010 with Kathleen. Out comes Clarice going to an invitation-only historical meeting in Nacogdoches, beautifully dressed and wearing her genuine cultured pearls. Thankfully, all of us have moved beyond white gloves. However, a cane or walker will never negate the need to wear pearls.

On another occasion at Clarice's house in Denton, Texas, around Christmas in early 1980, twelve of us were sitting around the dining room table, talking. Clarice was sharing how she had grown in the area of openness and directness. She now was able to get things out in the open more; no more sweeping things under the clean carpet.

As she talked, my neck began to get in a cramp because I was bending in to hear her. I looked around the table and we were all leaning in like we were in a football team huddle. Finally, I asked, "Why are you whispering, Clarice?" She answered, "Hamp's mother is visiting and I don't want her to hear me."

Clarice is the wife of a gynecologist—in fact one of three wives of gynecologists in the Spurs. I thought the "gyno trio," as I call them, would bring special knowledge about the mysteries of a woman's life. I never quite laid hold of the mysteries from any of them. The knowledge of female problems did not vanish; in fact it never appeared. Maybe I was not listening. My belief is that it was a southern lady type of conspiracy among all of them. They certainly had forthright husbands.

Recovery takes a lifetime, and the Spurs have had most of a lifetime together. Spurs are not followers, but still have been able to maintain a strong unity together in spite of our cultural and family traditions. Unity has high value in this group.

Left to right: Clarice Townes Miller, Pat Reynolds, Kathleen Page Clark.

Spurred by Grace
Chapter Three

A Time for Prayer

A Time for Miracles   by Gayle O'Neal
A Time to be Faithful   by Elizabeth Buckley
A Time to Bless   by Gayle O'Neal
A Time to Hang On   by Mimi Mack
A Time to Pray and Give Thanks   by Harriet Wallace

A Time for Miracles
Mountain Miracle
by Gayle O'Neal

Though I walk in the midst of trouble, you preserve my life;
you stretch out your hand against the anger of my foes,
with your right hand you save me.
The LORD will fulfill his purpose for me;
your love, O LORD, endures forever.......
Psalm 138:7-8 NIV 1984

"*C*ome quickly, send help! Zach has been struck by lightning! He isn't breathing; he's bleeding from his head! Please hurry! Please, please hurry."

These words sliced through a calm, beautiful and promising day of adventure for two teenage boys. Zach, my grandson who was fifteen, and Ernie, his friend who was sixteen, began this day with anticipation and excitement as they were going to climb West Spanish Peak, a 13,600 foot mountain in southeast Colorado.

Our family got up early that morning. The boys ate breakfast and packed a picnic lunch. At my insistence, they also packed my fully charged cell phone. My husband, Richard, and I (Zach's grandparents), along with Zach's mom and dad, drove the boys ten miles and walked with them two miles to the point where Zach and Ernie started their climb alone. We hurried back to our mountain condo to try to see the boys through a telescope on the deck—and we did! Zach's dad, Scott, zoomed in on two tiny pin-sized dots that jumped, separated and jumped again. We were awed that we could see them. It honestly looked like they were on the moon—a rugged, treeless terrain.

The day before, a park ranger, when asked, had given them two pieces of advised:

(1) Watch out for storms so go early in the morning, which they did—8:00 a.m.; and
(2) Watch for falling rocks.

Have you ever taken every precaution and yet things did not go as planned? Have you ever had a dream instantly turn into a nightmare?

When Zach and Ernie reached the peak, they built a rock cross at the top of the mountain. Before preparing to descend the mountain, the boys called on the cell phone exclaiming about the glorious beauty and incredible vistas from the very top of West Peak. Words like "awesome," "mind-boggling" and "beautiful" were pouring from them as they turned to view the valley from all angles and then—out of the blue—a bolt of lightning struck. It struck Zach in the back of his head burning off and frying his hair, destroying his clothes and shoes, exiting from several areas on his body and finally exiting out of his foot, leaving him with no heartbeat and a bleeding head wound.

The lightning went from Zach's body into the back of Ernie's thigh and exited through quarter-sized holes in Ernie's "brand new" shoes.

The boys were stranded at the top of the mountain and in the middle of a lightning rainstorm—dangerously injured, wet and extremely chilled. "Send help—come now, please hurry!" were the words we heard from Ernie on the cell phone.

Scott, Zach's dad, grabbed a motorcycle. Miraculously, this motorcycle had not run in two years and just two days before, Zach and his dad had gotten it to run! Scott did not know if his son were dead or alive but he began a three-hour journey to find these boys. He wanted to keep from becoming a tragedy himself because the roads were slick and dangerous. Continual prayers were pouring out of his heart. "Oh God, Oh God, please!"

Meanwhile the three of us (Zach's mom, my husband and I) were in the car driving the longest ten miles of our lives. Prayers were pouring forth from our hearts and mouths. Was Zach dead or alive? How would these two boys get down that treacherous mountain? What shape would they be in? "Oh God, please!"

Mollie, Zach's thirteen-year-old sister, and her friend Alisa were left back at the condo asking these same questions and for five hours they waited and waited, knowing nothing.

Thank God for cell phones! I knew instinctively to immediately call the Spurs and get them to pray. The Spurs have always been there for each other, and heaven knows, I needed them now.

My husband Richard was continuously on his cell phone with Ernie. The cell phone they had taken was still miraculously working after the lightning strike. Ernie was terrified and feeling very close to panic when he remembered "CPR." He began to beat on Zach's chest—thank you God for this young man—and Richard heard Zach begin to moan. We recognized his moans and knew for the first time he was alive.

Scott's journey is another incredible story. Scott, Zach's dad, did not know that Zach was still alive and he did not know for about another two hours. He did make it up to the trailhead, but the motorcycle could go no further. Scott began climbing up on jagged rocks—no trails, no air! He kept waiting for the adrenalin surge but it never came, so he staggered and staggered. Scott is very strong and very fit but this was almost impossible. He struggled to keep going but kept falling back.

Then, Scott told us later, he thought he saw a man, whom he believed must be Jesus or one of His angels, on the mountain. A peace immediately came over him. He kept climbing and after a while, scanning the mountain he saw two tiny specs he thought were moving. Could it be them? His energy was revived and after a seeming eternity he could see two figures. "Oh God, could it be? Could it be? It is!"

Meanwhile, on the top of the mountain, Zach regained consciousness. He was totally addled and confused. Ernie told him they had to wait for help. There was freezing rain. Zach was terribly burned. His clothing that had not been melted to his skin was beginning to blow off. Zach told Ernie that he was feeling terrible and that they had to try to go down the mountain.

The boys agreed that before they went down they had to pray. Ernie said they prayed, "Dear God, if you want to take us now that's okay—but if you don't, you have to help us get down this mountain."

Now, how would they get down? Zach's shoes were destroyed and he kept struggling to walk in what was left of the shoes. Ernie, seeing his struggle, gave Zach his good shoe (Zach wears size 12, Ernie wears size 8-1/2). Then the gutsiest, most heroic descent began.

Richard (my husband and Zach's grandfather) told Ernie to watch for the headlights of Scott's motorcycle. After about two hours, Ernie finally saw the headlights. As we talked to him on the phone, we could hear the hope and relief in his voice. Richard kept saying, "Scott is coming—Scott is coming!"

Meanwhile, Zach's mom, Richard and I were at the trailhead watching the EMT's ascent up the mountain and listening to the helicopter pilot talking on his radio. The boys were too high and there was no place to land.

Would this day ever end? I knew there were severe injuries but we had to play the waiting game. The volunteers were so wonderful, trying to help us as this day dragged on. We were in shock, but I took comfort in knowing the Spurs were praying.

Finally, the helicopter pilot circled higher up the mountain and was able to land in a small meadow. Zach was quickly boarded after all the precautions were taken to protect his wounds. He was flown to Pueblo, Colorado—another provision by God and was in ICU three days before he was out of danger. The boys quickly became heroes and were given new names— "Sparky and Smokey." People knew that God, in His mercy, had spared their lives.

Finally Scott, with Ernie on the back of his motorcycle, arrived at the trailhead where we were waiting. Scott was also carrying Zach's shredded and melted clothes that smelled like burnt flesh. After about four hours of not knowing anything, his first words to us were, "He's alive. Zach is alive."

The lightning strike occurred at noon and they were down at 5:30 p.m. As I looked up at the mountain, it was now completely obscured by the storm.

I do not understand why all of this happened and I do not understand why Zach has eyes, a brain, or even hair. I don't understand why he can still think or talk or walk. I truly do not understand the mercy of our great and merciful God who works His mercy in many different ways. This I do know: We will soak in His goodness and His mercy. We will continue to thank Him and marvel at how great and mighty is our God!

Thank you, Lord.
Thank you, Spurs.

This is not just Ernie and Zach's story.
This is God's story.

They also have a new appreciation for this biblical promise:

"....For I know the plans I have for you," declares the LORD, "plans to prosper you and not to harm you, plans to give you a hope and a future. Then you will call on me and come and pray to me, and I will listen to you...."
Jeremiah 29:11-12

Gayle O'Neal holding grandson Zack's jeans
after he was struck by lightning.

A Time to be Faithful
He is Faithful
by Elizabeth Buckley

For I proclaim the name of the LORD;
Ascribe greatness to our God!
The Rock! His work is perfect, for all His ways are justice.
A God of faithfulness and without injustice,
Righteous and upright is He.
Deuteronomy 32:3-4 (NASB)

From the first time the Spurs met in 1977 for a retreat led by Pat Reynolds on Psalm 23, we have been faithfully bonded to each other. A connection was made that weekend that has lasted thirty-five years, as of this writing. The teaching was wonderful and challenged us to go deeper in the Lord. Our time of getting to know one another was so refreshing because we let down our guards and were just "girls" being real. All that was great, but God had an even greater plan. He created an elegant tapestry by weaving our lives together and adding many more "girls" to that work of art as the years went by.

I love all the Spurs: the variety of personalities, ages, church affiliations, marital status, etc. The quality which has been consistent in all of us is faithfulness. In the book of Revelation 19:11, it says that on the thigh of Jesus is written "Faithful and True." Many times in the scriptures the word "faith" is actually "faithfulness" as in Habakkuk 2:4 "But, the righteous will live by his faith/faithfulness." (NASB) It is true that we love because God first loved us and gave His Son, Jesus, to die for our sins. It is also true that we have learned faithfulness because He is faithful. No matter what we have had to go through in our individual lives, this precious group of women has traveled the road together. We have supported one another through death, murder, divorce, depression, sickness, joy, salvation, weddings, births, all the things life brings, and we have remained faithful to God and faithful to each other.

So, for my part in this book, I have written this prayer:

> *Dear Father,*
> *Oh, how we love You. We love You, Lord. You have proved Your love and steadfastness to us over and over. We give You honor for all You have done in our lives, and for all You are going to do. We know that we belong to You, our Creator. You laid down Your life for us so that we can be eternally with You. You have taught us faithfulness because You are faithful. It is Your faithfulness, not our own, on which we depend and it is Your faithfulness which will carry us to the end. Just as You loved us to the end (See John 13:1), so shall we love You to the end. We long for the day when we will see You face-to-face. Lord, we are Yours.*
> *Amen.*

A Time to Bless

by Gayle O'Neal

*And we know that in all things God works
for the good of those who love him,
who have been called according to his purpose.
Romans 8:28*

One of our three sons went through a devastating divorce. The wife and children left, taking much of the furniture with them. The house that had been their home for ten years was now vacant, cold and emptied—furnishings and family gone.

My son and I hustled to fill in the empty spaces and make it look like a home again.

It was then that the Spurs descended with joy, laughter, life and gratitude to gather with him to bless his home. We gathered in the entry of the home and each offered sentence prayers, like the Spurs often do.

The Spurs circle up to pray.

We then gathered outside in front of the house and took a very meaningful group photo because so many of us were there.

The home and his life have been restored and blessed. Truly blessed.

This is an example of what the Spurs are about and do so well.

The Spurs gather to bless the home of one of Gayle O'Neal's sons.

Left to right standing: Carolyn Boyd, Phyllis White, Sandra Talkington, Mimi Mack, Pat Reynolds, Sally Renshaw, Georgia Smith, Maureen Eagan, Clarice Townes Miller, Barbara Clarkin.

Left to right seated: Harriet Wallace, Mary Alice Brumley, Molly Dummit, Gayle O'Neal, Elizabeth Buckley, Kathleen Page Clark.

A Time to Hang On
A Tragedy and a Miracle
by Mimi Mack

".....For I know the plans I have for you," declares the LORD,
"plans to prosper you and not to harm you,
plans to give you hope and a future......"
Jeremiah 29:11

On March 19, 2010, my husband, Jerry, and his dear friend, Tom Zachry, met early in the morning for a day of fishing. It is their passionate hobby and both were very excited. In fact, Tom was so anxious to get started, he called to ask if Jerry could meet an hour earlier than planned!

Tom, a successful, longtime lawyer, had just been elected Judge and they were celebrating his achievement of a dream come true. He was an honorable man, full of integrity and compassion.

They drove to Lake Aquilla in central Texas. Tom brought his boat, so they launched it and started fishing. Two happy men! Around 11 a.m., the temperature started dropping with very strong winds. The waves shortly became tabletop high. They knew they needed to head for shore! However, the boat was having some mechanical problems, so it was very slow going. The high waves and winds made it a fight every foot toward shore. About 11:45 a.m., a large wave flipped the boat and threw both men out. They were able to swim back to the overturned boat and hang on. There were no other boats in the area to help. The water was ice cold. The waves were pounding them continually as the temperature continued to drop because an ice storm was on its way. They were a long way from shore and swimming would be almost impossible in the fierce, high waves. After two and a half hours of constant pounding and cold, Tom made the decision to swim rather than freeze. He felt very confident he would make it. Jerry had already made the decision to wait until 6:00 p.m. for a boat to come. If not, he would also try to swim to shore. Tom's mind was made up and he couldn't wait any longer so he started swimming. He swam about thirty-five yards and went under. He did not resurface. What a terrible, heart-wrenching sight! A precious friend—gone! Tom wasn't found for six days—a devastating wait for all of us.

After Tom was gone, my husband pictured in his mind sitting in our home, as we do every morning, drinking coffee, holding the cat, and talking with me. He also told himself, "I will not die; I will be home again." He was so strong and God was so faithful as he never was fearful or anxious. His decision was to swim at 6:00 p.m. while it was still light, and until then, he would see how tough he was.

God's miracle showed up at 5:45 p.m. in the form of another boat and two young men who rescued him. He was suffering from severe hypothermia and was practically incoherent. He could not help himself, so the two young men (God's angels) lifted him into their boat, called 911 and headed for the boat ramp. When they reached the boat ramp, the two young men had to lift him again, this time from the boat onto the dock. This was no easy task as he weighed 250 pounds and is 6 feet, 4 inches tall. God had two more angels fishing on the ramp already in place to help. A woman took Jerry's wet shirt off and put her dry shirt and jacket on him. When the ambulance arrived, his body temperature had dropped to 90 degrees, which is as low as it can get before death. The situation could have gone either way at this point. The 911 team was wonderful, wrapping him in blankets and rushing him to Lake Whitney Hospital emergency room where two more angels took over in the form of nurses. Hypothermia causes the body and organs to shut down. So, although they had him under heated blankets that blew hot air on him, it took over an hour for his temperature to move up to 91 degrees. His veins had shrunk, so it was several hours before they could start an IV. It was very serious.

I was home innocently preparing dinner and expecting him home. I had a phone call about 6:15 p.m. from the hospital:

"Mrs. Mack, has anyone called you about your husband? He has been in a very serious boating accident and is in the emergency room. Can you come?"

"Yes, yes, I will come, of course I will come, but what about his friend? There were two men fishing together."

"I'm sorry. They only brought one man in here. There was no one else," the nurse replied.

"May I please speak to my husband?"

"He is very incoherent, but I will put the phone to his ear."

"Jerry, honey," I began, "tell me where Tom is......."

One word: "Drowned."

"I am coming! Please, please, hang on," I said.

I hung up, called two dear friends, (a Spur and her husband), told them what happened and to please go to Tom's wife, Marilyn, and be with her. She wasn't called by the Sheriff until after 9:00 p.m., so my friends had the heartbreaking task of telling her what had happened to Tom.

I ran to my car and started driving, sobbing so hard I could hardly see. My cell phone rang, and this time, God had sent me an angel! It was a close friend that gently talked me into calming down and focusing on driving safely. She made all the difference in that drive. I was then able to pray and concentrate on my job, which was to get to Jerry. Shortly, I pulled over long enough to call my son, Scott, in Colorado. He immediately said, "I've got it, Mom, just drive." What confidence I had knowing that he could and would do everything that needed to be done. He called the hospital, he talked to the doctor, called my son, Jamie, and called me back to say, "Dad will live and Jamie is on his way to the hospital from Bryan." My daughter, Kristi, and her family were on a family ski trip staying with Scott in Colorado. Scott and Kristi packed hurriedly and drove through a blizzard to get to the hospital and their Dad the next morning. After they arrived, they took over all the hospital duties. We are so proud of them. What loving care he had!

I haven't been able to drive at night for several years because of my vision. The long empty country roads were pitch dark that March night in 2010—no lights, no houses, no signs, and yet God opened my eyes and I could see perfectly. I came to a "Y" in the road where I had been told there was a large sign to the hospital. There was no sign, but there was a small service station. I went in to ask directions and said, "My husband has been in a boating accident and I need to get to the hospital. I am lost." Behind me in line was another angel that said, "Honey, follow me, I will take you there," which she did.

Finally, at the hospital, I looked up and standing outside in the cold at the front door was my precious friend, Deanna. I couldn't believe my eyes. How I thank God for her!

As I walked into the hospital, what a God-given surprise it was to find that seven of our closest friends had already driven from Fort Worth to be with us. My dear Lord had **everything** in place for Jerry and for me. What a loving support team we had! Prayers by the hundreds had already started continually going up. When my son, Jamie, walked into the hospital one hour later, it was another gift from God. He was the angel I needed the most right then. Jamie is a fireman and is so capable, efficient and gentle. He spent that first night talking to the doctors, nurses and Sheriff—and continually encouraging all of us. Jamie is the one who made the arrangements to move Jerry by ambulance to a bigger, better-equipped hospital the next morning.

Jerry's temperature continued to rise very slowly. His body had put a huge amount of toxic enzymes into his system and his kidneys were functioning abnormally. He remained in the hospital for a week with caring nurses and doctors giving excellent care. I learned from them how serious my husband's condition was. His doctor told him, "You have a strong soul, Mr. Mack—a **very** strong soul."

My blessed children stayed with me, doing everything possible—checking the blood work, talking to doctors and being very protective of me. To this day, they continue to stand close by, anticipating our needs, and are ready to help. How blessed we are!

As I think back on that dreadful time, I cannot doubt that God was there every minute in every way from the time the boat overturned until today. I not only believe in miracles, I saw them visibly in the people and circumstances constantly. Jerry is getting better and stronger each day. Tom's wife is nobly walking a very hard path. I love her and admire her courage in this heartbreaking situation. My heart aches for her. Tom would be so proud of her, as we all are!

I will miss Tom every day for the rest of my life and be humbly grateful that I still have the love of my life, Jerry, my husband of fifty-four years. Tom loved our Lord and is in Heaven, a better place. We will all be reunited in Heaven someday. A miracle and an earthly tragedy for his family occurred that stormy day but God's loving presence was in all of it.

Jeremiah 29:11 has been my prayer throughout. What a beautiful promise! What a gracious God!

Jerry Mack, holding a prize catch, prior to his
serious boating accident while fishing.

A Time to Pray and Give Thanks

by Harriet Wallace

All your children will be taught by the LORD,
and great will be their peace.
Isaiah 54:13

Introduction

These are the prayers that I pray for my children and grand-children and share with my Spur friends. As you intercede for your children, grandchildren and great-grandchildren, my prayer for you is that the Holy Spirit will lead, guide and direct you to His promises pertaining to your concerns for them that He promises to perfect.

Prayer

Father, thank you for giving us the gift of children. We have brought them up in the way that they should go. We pray that they will not depart from it. We pray that they will make You the Lord of their lives and that they will not lean on their own understanding, but in all their ways acknowledge You and do everything as unto the Lord.

Father, thank you for the good work that You have started in our children's lives. I pray that You will perfect that work until that day of Jesus Christ. I pray that they will walk in a manner worthy of the Lord, to please Him in all respects, bearing fruit in every good work and increasing in the knowledge of God. Father, please keep our children as the apple of Your eye and hide them under the shadow of Your wings.

Father, I pray that our children will always honor their mother and father so that all will be well with them. May they always listen to their father's instruction, and never forsake their mother's teaching. Cause them to look not only to their own interests, but also to the interest of others. Lord, please give them a servant's heart and help their attitudes to always be the same as that of Christ Jesus.

Father, You said You planned for our children before the foundation of the earth, that you knew them before they were formed in the womb, and that You have plans for them for good and not evil. Please help them to always keep in their remembrance that their bodies are the temple of the Holy Spirit, that they are not their own but have been bought with a price and therefore are to glorify God in their bodies.

Father, I pray that our children will seek the Kingdom of God first, and all the other things will be added unto them. Help them not to be anxious for anything because in the Kingdom they will have joy and peace. I pray that they will know that You are the God of all comfort, You will provide according to your riches in glory and You will perfect all the things that concern them.

Father, I pray that our children will always have a teachable spirit. May they value their relationship with You and continue to hunger and thirst after righteousness and intimacy with You, so that they may know Your love that surpasses all understanding.

Father, give our children a spirit of discernment so that they will make the right choices. Help them to be kind, tenderhearted and forgiving just as God in Christ has forgiven them. May they always follow Jesus and be a blessing wherever they go.

Father, I pray that as the days of our children's lives increase, they will grow as Jesus grew, becoming strong in their spirit and filled with grace and favor. Please give them deep and clear knowledge of Your will in all spiritual wisdom and understanding and discernment of spiritual things. May they come to know the Holy Spirit as their Comforter, Counselor, Helper, Advocate, Intercessor, Strengthener, Teacher and Standby.

Thank you, Father, that Your Word says that our ability to succeed is based on our knowledge and understanding of Your Word. I pray that our children will meditate on Your Word and observe to do all that is written in it so that they may make their way prosperous and have good success. Oh, that their testimony would be "I have better understanding and deeper insight than all my teachers, because Your testimonies are my meditation."

Father, just as You had a hedge of protection around Israel, Your covenant people, please put a hedge of protection around our children so that they cannot find their way to wrong places or wrong people and wrong people cannot find their way to them. Father, please let no weapon formed against them prosper and any tongue that accuses them in judgment, condemn. Thank you for the promise that You would go before our children and please remind them that you have not given them the spirit of fear, but of power and love and a sound mind.

Father, thank you that you will protect the seeds of faith that have been planted in our children. Protect their minds and hearts each day. Fill their minds with Your light and Your truth. Protect them as they travel and wherever they lay their heads. Hide them in the shelter of Your wings from all harm. Be for them an encircling wall of fire. May the light of Your glory shine around them and within them and within every place of their habitations to keep them safe in Your presence. Thank you, Lord, that you are their Shepherd, that they will never want, and goodness and mercy will follow them all the days of their lives.

Father, I pray that you would keep our children from any sort of substitute that would take first place in their lives before You. Help them to avoid loving anything or anyone more than You. May You always be to them, their first love.

Thank you, Father, for the promise of safety and ease every day for our children, and for the angels that are given special charge over them to accompany, defend, and preserve them. Father, may they find favor, good understanding and high esteem in Your sight and in the sight of man. Oh, Father, that they would be disciples taught of the Lord and obedient to Your will. May they have great peace and undisturbed composure.

Father, I pray that our children will hear only the voice of the Good Shepherd so that they may stand firmly on the Word of God and not be influenced by enticing words and things of the world. May Your law be written on their hearts that they may not slip. May they have great peace so that they will not stumble, and fear of the Lord that is pleasing in Your sight.

Father, I thank you for the promise that our children will not be tempted beyond their strength. That along with the tests they encounter, You will give them a way out of it so that they may be able to endure it. Thank you that You are making them strong in their inner being. Keep their hearts tender, their conscience sensitive, and their eyes always on the One who never slumbers or sleeps so that He may keep them from evil and guard their coming in and going out from this time forth and forever.

Father, I pray that our children will always have hearts of greatfulness, that they will always remember that every good and perfect gift comes from their Father above, and that they will never take anything for granted. May their hearts continually overflow with great thanksgiving and humility for all that You do for and through them.

Father, thank you that our children are becoming great men and women of God who exalts and highly esteem Your Word. Thank you that they will make Your Word the final authority to settle all questions that confront them. Thank you that their hearts are fixed and established in the living Word of God.

Father, we commit our children into Your keeping and know that they are blessed by You all the days of their lives. You have inscribed their names on the palms of Your hands and promise never to forget them, but to guide them until death.

In Jesus' name, we pray.

Amen

Spurred by Grace
Chapter Four

A Time for Friendship

A Time to Write a Hurting Friend

(A love letter to a hurting Spur)

by Mimi Mack

Keep ourselves wrapped up in God's love
as we wait for the mercy of Christ to bring
those we love to eternal life.
Jude 1:21 (paraphrased by Mimi)

While the Spurs were on a trip to Italy, the father of one of the Spurs on the trip died and her mother was very ill. Here is a letter written from one Spur to another:

June 30, 1998

Precious Phyllis,

I remember standing by our Villa in Italy with the Spurs in the barren vineyard on that sad Sunday your father died. How empty, hopeless and dead it all seemed as we looked at those dry, brown grapevines. You were feeling just like those vines that day—and now, once again, you find yourself in that dry, hard and hopeless place. My earnest and heartfelt prayers are going "up" continually for you and your mom. The two of you are in the palm of God's hand and wrapped around His heart so tightly that He can't and won't take His eyes off you for one second. You are His own dear child and have His undivided attention. You probably don't "feel" it right now, so just trust that it is true (because He has promised) and keep this pictured in your mind until you begin to feel it.

Remember the lush green, growing grape vines before we left Italy? What a reminder of the loving, merciful heart of God! Jude 1:21 (paraphrased by Mimi) reminds us to keep ourselves wrapped up in God's love as we wait for the mercy of Christ to bring those we love to eternal life.

It is life, abundant life, ahead for your mom—not death. What a sweet reunion she will have with your dad while all the angels will be cheering her into Heaven!

I am so grateful for our Lord's promises that you can know with absolute confidence of your mom's happy future.

However, we are down here and it's hard to watch and let go, so my heart is aching for you! I am asking God to remove your mother's physical pain and give her a peaceful rest for whatever time she has left. I'm asking God to heal your broken heart and give you encouragement as only He can give. If I could, I would jump in and fill up that great big hole in your heart. Of course I can't, so I am asking our Lord to do just that and also hug you so tight that you even begin to feel it.

1 Peter 5:10 promises:

> ....that the God of all grace, who called you to his eternal glory in Christ, after you have suffered a little while, will himself restore you and make you strong, firm and steadfast.

Try to picture Jesus and the angels standing all around her bed waiting to walk her to Heaven. Then try to picture your many friends on their knees praying and waiting to put their hand in yours to walk with you in whatever is ahead.

Many love you so much and I'm standing at the front of the line!

You are my precious friend,
Mimi

P.S. I gave you this grapevine in Italy—so I give it to you again to remind you of joyful times ahead and the ultimate purpose of God's pruning.

Left to right: Phyllis White, Mary Alice Brumley, Mimi Mack.

A Time to Sing
The Porch Swing
by Mary Alice Brumley

We who had sweet fellowship together....
Psalm 55:14 (NASB)

There has always been a porch swing in my life, as long as I can remember. As a little child, I thought it was the very best way to spend a summer afternoon with my grandmother. We would sit in the swing together on the front porch of her home and watch as the world went by. Without speaking a word, we had the best conversation ever as the swing moved to and fro and she held me in her arms. We would swing until the fireflies came out to play at dusk signaling that it was time for her to go in and start dinner.

I remember a time when I was visiting in Colorado with the Spurs. I was sitting in a porch swing with my friend, Molly, singing old hymns. We were both deeply moved as we looked out over the majestic purple mountains and drank in their beauty and strength. The Lord's spirit poured over us as we swayed back and forth praising God with our voices. It was uplifting and refreshing, like a cool breeze whispering across the depths of our souls.

Now that I am a grandmother, I long for times to sit, reflect and be quiet and swing. I look for opportunities to do this with my grandchildren. I can chase away their fears or share a story or two of years gone by as we hold hands and listen to each other's dreams. I never grow weary of being a part of their world.

I asked my husband what came to mind when he thought of a porch swing. He immediately said, "Romance." It seems we are all looking for love and security, whether it's swinging to and fro in the arms of your grandmother; or sitting next to a cherished friend singing praises to God; or holding hands and swinging to your heart's content with your grandchildren; or chasing a kiss from your sweetheart. Important things happen on the porch in a swing with someone you love nestled next to you. It is a time of sweet fellowship that makes your heart sing!

A Time for Hospitality

by Anne Hyde

Keep on loving each other as brothers and sisters.
Don't forget to show hospitality to strangers,
for some who have done this have entertained angels
without realizing it!
Hebrews 13:1-2 (NLT)

When I think of the years of joy and comfort that the Spurs have meant to me, I first think of laughter they have brought to my home. When we were first building our beautiful home and just the framing was up, the Spurs came to pray for our family and new home to be filled with joy. It was very cold, and we were all bundled up and filled with laughter at our red noses and shivering cold breath.

For many years that home became a place of hospitality for the Spurs. There were wedding showers, baby showers, regular meetings, missionary meetings, and on one joyous occasion, a slumber party. My daughter, Annie Laurie, asked, "Who are these Spurs? Rodeo Queens?" We all laughed. Annie Laurie played the guitar and we sang for hours.

What wonderful memories!

Left to right: Pat Reynolds, Anne Hyde.

A Time for Loyalty

by Pat Reynolds

A friend is always loyal,
and a brother is born to help in time of need.
Proverbs 17:17 (NLT)

There are "friends" who destroy each other,
but a real friend sticks closer than a brother.
Proverbs 18:24 (NLT)

Loyalty: faithful allegiance to a person, group or cause. (Merriam-Webster)

There is a time in life when one needs to KNOW by expressed words and actions that you have loyalty from selected friends.

The wonderfulness for me through the years is the family aspect of the Spurs. I had come from a small family—my brother and myself. My brother had been a functional alcoholic for years, so there was no closeness. I have one other cousin. Other than my children and their children, I am alone. Bob's three sisters live in North Dakota—a different culture and far away from where we live in Texas.

I feel so close to many of the Spurs that I know I would be welcomed at their Christmas table. The Spurs provide me with family. I am not alone. The Holy Father has made provision for me through the Spurs.

*Father to the fatherless, defender of widows—this is God,
whose dwelling is holy. God places the lonely in families...*
    Psalm 68:5-6 (NLT)

*Even if my father and mother abandon me, the Lord will
hold me close.*
    Psalm 27:10 (NLT)

I have been "took up" by the Spurs. The Spurs have been a family that sticks by me. See 2 Cor. 1:3-4 (NLT) and 1 Thess. 2:7-8 (NLT).

In a family, there comes a time when you must have loyalty even when you know you have blown it. My time had come. I came from a family where loyalty was conditional and you didn't know the "present" conditions. I needed the loyalty that "sticks with or sticks up," or you might say a loyalty that would be "stuck on me."

I remember going down the Spur list to see whom I could count on—who would be in and who would be out. I had seen snippets of loyalty through the years for others, but for me, let's see. Of course this was about my early family experiences.

At one of the Spur meetings, a Spur was talking about a woman she was forgiving who could have potentially damaged her family. Well, one of the sweetest Spurs said, "I am going to pull her hair out." Another biblically astute Spur was going to "scratch her eyes out." So maybe this group, or some in the group, had the goods for me.

You need loyalty when you are wrong, right, righteous or unrighteous. I am not talking about a loyalty that condones per-petuating wrongdoing. I am talking about loyalty in our human frailty and insufficient understanding. In this situation I was in, I had unintentionally been good, bad, smart, dumb, righteous and unrighteous. I needed the Spurs to stick "closer than a brother" or really, a sister in Jesus.

Loyalty in the Spurs does not mean supporting wrong behavior and attitudes. It means walking alongside, giving you comfort, understanding and protection—I call this staying power—until you get to the place God wants you to be. You don't lose the family (Spurs) in the process. Our society is so in and out, and emotionally mobile. Can't stick. Can't stay.

Now came the loyalty Spur test: Do you get loyalty whether you deserve it or not? I didn't perform well. I made some mistakes and I had good intentions but made bad choices. There were two Spurs in particular that I needed to know were loyal because they were involved in the situation: Kathleen and Molly.

First on my list was Kathleen. We were both at a New Year's retreat at Laity Lodge. I expressed my dilemma, thinking I might lose her. She would have to make a choice. She was surprised, and I think a little hurt, that I would think she would fail the test. Kathleen is a fairness person (just let her balance your travel money!). Her loyalty that I needed might not seem fair or reasonable to her. Hold your breath, Pat! She came through with flying colors in a "fairness way" that was loyal to me.

Left to right: Kathleen Page Clark, Pat Reynolds.

Now came test number two: At seven o'clock one morning, after driving fifty miles, I called Molly on my cell phone and said I wanted to have coffee with her. She asked, "Well, where are you, Pat?" To her surprise, I replied, "I am in your driveway." That morning, I said, "Molly, this is what I need whether it makes sense to you or not. I need your loyalty in this situation. Will you give it to me?" She responded wholeheartedly, "Yes." I now know that all I needed to do was ask. I am grateful the Spurs have become a safe place for me to ask for help!

After all my years with the Spurs, I discovered that they could pass my test. I now feel secure in their loyalty.

Ask and you shall receive.

A Time to Love
The Gift of Love
by Mary Alice Brumley

The sacrifices of God are a broken spirit;
A broken and a contrite heart, O God, You will not despise.
Psalm 51:17 (NASB)

*O*ut of brokenness flows blessing. The gift of love came from a broken heart. God gave His only Son to die for our sins and it was the best gift of love that has ever been given. God is love and without Him there is no love. He loved us too much to leave us in the condition that we were in or to leave us without love.

I have experienced God's love in many ways. The more we experience God's love, the more love we have to give. One of the gifts of love that He has given me is through the Spurs. The purpose of our group is to spur one another on to good works, which follows scripture. My prayer is that I would allow the love of Christ to control me as it says in 2 Corinthians 5:14-15 (NASB).

For the love of Christ controls us, having concluded this, that one died for all, therefore all died; and He died for all, so that they who live might no longer live for themselves, but for Him who died and rose again on their behalf.

Wow! That is such a wonderful way to live. The apostle Paul went from terrorizing and abusing people to ministering and loving them. I believe that God is a God of restoration and that He is able to restore us to Himself to bring glory to Him.

When I became a part of the Spurs, I had been broken by divorce. I had remarried but I still needed a friend. I got more than I bargained for with the Spurs, because I got a whole room full of friends who would listen to me, pray for me and love me. The Spurs strengthened me because they gave me a safe place to just sit and listen and to know that I was not the only one with problems. It was a place where I could learn to be whole again without feeling like I was letting someone down by my own weaknesses. They gave me the time to heal so that I could courageously face the world again and be a blessing of love to others.

I am still learning that I am always in the center of God's love, no matter what my circumstances happen to be. What a blessing it has been to walk through life with these friends who have faced so many heartbreaking challenges and who have the gift of God's love in their hearts. I know that I will someday be spending eternity with them and in a perfect place, no less! We will still be laughing, singing and sharing together but there will be no more tears. I cherish each friendship that I have made in the Spurs because I know that I can trust them with my heart. None of us knows what tomorrow will bring, but I know that love will take me there with Jesus and my friends who will be there to "spur" me on!

Mary Alice Brumley

A Time to be Sisters
In life and death!
by Maureen Eagan

And stretching out his hand toward his disciples, he said,
"Here are my mother and my brothers!
For whoever does the will of my
Father in heaven is my brother, and SISTER, and mother."
Matthew 12:49-50 (ESV) Caps are by the author of this story.

They came up the front walk to my granddaughter Molly's house in single file, nine or ten women. One carried a huge bouquet of all white flowers. As my granddaughter's husband, Coby, opened the door, he looked at this group of attractive older women with some surprise while one of them announced, "We're the Spurs!" All of them had driven at least thirty miles, and some fifty, to be present with us during an evening family visitation following grandson Zach's private graveside service.

Another Spur, Clarice, had previously driven one and a half hours to be present for the Memorial Service for my eighteen-year-old grandson, Zach Eagan in Shreveport, Louisiana. Clarice and her husband, Hamp, my daughter Caren, Zach's aunt and one other family were the only ones we knew from outside the Shreveport area. Clarice's face was so welcome as were the flowers she placed on the table that was filled with picture albums.

I truly felt that one of my sisters was with me.

Not quite two years earlier, the Spurs came for the graveside service of my son, Rex Eagan, (Zach's father, 54), who, like Zach, had died too young!

Eighteen years earlier the Spurs were present at the memorial service for my husband, Woody, who died at sixty-seven. At Woody's memorial, they completely filled a pew two rows behind where the family was seated. I turned at one point to see them all there and immediately thought of God's words, "I will be your rear guard!" They were there to cover my vulnerability, and to share my sorrow and loss! They were there!

Now more about the big white bouquet: I placed it on my dining table, which is literally in the center of my house! There must have been seven or eight different kinds of flowers, all white, and with greenery. Among those flowers were fragrant lilies, roses, snapdragons, mums, carnations, butterfly gladiolas and gorgeous greenery, so representative of the different Spurs, so generous and unique. The fragrance filled the whole house, and the buds just kept blooming—for almost ten days!

During that time it was as if their presence were with me—gently reminding me of their care, shared sorrow and faithfulness.

Even more significant, was a revelation and realization as I looked at the pure white petals, that everything in Heaven is going to be pure! What must that be like to be completely surrounded by purity? Your love is purified, your body is purified, your thoughts are purified, your vision is purified (now we see in a mirror darkly, but then we shall see face to face), and your emotions and intentions are purified. So for days I reveled in the fact that Woody's (my husband's) heavenly body is cancer free, Rex's (my son's) heavenly body does not have diseased lungs or heart, and Zach's (my grandson's) body does not have a poisoned appendix and is heavenly normal.

Woody never got to see Zach. He was born six weeks after Woody's death. Recently on what would have been Woody's eighty-fifth birthday, I envisioned Rex and Zach with their beautiful voices not only praising God, purely, but singing Happy Birthday to Woody.

It is a blessed thing to share with my Spur sisters that not only are our loved ones in "a better place," but they are in the "best place!"

A Time to Thank

(on behalf of all the Spurs)

by Kathleen Page Clark

I thank my God upon every remembrance of you.......
Philippians 1:3 (KJV)

$\mathcal{P}$at Reynolds is often our Spur facilitator. With God-given wisdom she has helped to keep our group together. She has guided us through times of conflict, discord and difficulty. Insight and maturity have been gained and shared by all. We wanted to do something really significant to express our gratitude for all she had done (and continues to do) for the Spurs as a group and as individuals. There is not a single Spur that has not been significantly impacted by her love and counsel.

It had been a lifelong dream of Pat's to go to Israel, so the Spurs made that happen! Here is the poem that was read when we presented her this gift.

A Poem and Love Gift to Express our Thanks

Pat, my dear, it is way past time,
For the Spurs to put our thanks in rhyme.
We thank our God that He made you.
Without our Pat, what would we do?

You have led us, counseled us, and housed us all.
But more than that, as I recall;
Our sons and daughters are blessed as well.
At loving and counseling you do excel.

Thank you for your years of wisdom and insight.
You have led us with laughter and such delight.
Words of thanks are nice to say,
But we wanted to do more, in a different way.

With thankful hearts, an envelope we passed.
We collected a love gift, oh so fast!
Our thanks to you we wanted to show.
We hope in February to Israel you'll go!

Written by Kathleen Page Elliott
Read on October 25, 1998 in Pineville, Missouri

Needless to say, there were tears of gratitude and lots of hugs!

A Time for Receiving and Giving

by Pat Reynolds

Freely you have received; freely give.
Matthew 10:8

During my life with the Spurs, I have been active in four different churches within three different denominations. My circles of relationships change around me, but the Spurs have been a constant, providing an anchor to learn how to experience trust so I can give and receive love and acceptance.

Everyone is looking for someone to love them, but I contend that giving love that is received is as powerful as receiving love that is given.

I remember being involved with a foster teenager who had no family. The agency responsible for him gave him gifts for Christmas, but he had no one to give gifts to. Our Heavenly Father knows the power of giving love (as He gave us His Son) that is received.

My primary family didn't let you love them easily. The Spurs have been and are a place where I could love them and their children. They would receive it whether my heart was perfect or not.

I get the sense that the Spurs think I gave them more than they give me, but I have always felt that they gave me more than I give them. I think that's another one of the mysteries of the Spurs; you feel you get more than you give.

On one occasion I did get more for sure. The Spurs decided that I had given "free counseling" for years and they truly surprised me by giving me a trip to Israel.

I am so grateful for these years with them. Knowing that I belonged, I could learn how to trust so I could receive and give love.

Spurred by Grace
Chapter Five

A Time for Healing

A Time to Say Goodbye
The Silent Goodbye
by Mary Alice Brumley

And she smiles at the future.
Proverbs 31:25 (NASB)

J felt an overwhelming sadness during his illness and death. There was an ache deep within me that I could not touch. The pain divided my soul. At his funeral, it seemed as if I were on a stage. Part of my life was playing out before me but I was not allowed to speak. I was there but it was like I was invisible. I was watching but I was not in the play. It was like a silent goodbye when you are waving to a loved one who is already on the train. I was waving goodbye but no one could hear what I was saying. All I could do was wave. I was not involved in the drama.

I never wanted to erase the years we were married or pretend they hadn't happened. I wanted to remember the very essence of knowing him and how we fell in love. I wanted my children to know about the wonderful times we spent together as a couple, and that I was proud that he was their father. After all, it was our love that had given them life and what a gift that had been for us. Our first-born son was our pride and joy, as were all our children. No two people could have shared any more joy together than the two of us as we shared our children's lives.

So much has happened in my life since we divorced. The memories have grown dimmer with each passing year. I had to make myself go on living after the death of our marriage. Now I found myself facing the reality of what his death really meant to me after all these years of living without him. Would the memories sustain me and keep my emotions at bay? Would I be able to walk back into the past without losing the freedom that I had found by living in the present? Could I ever forget how desperately incapable I felt when I had to go on living without him?

Death brings finality to all of us in one way or another. My emotions were tangled with feelings of anger, rejection, separation, loneliness, fear, love, misunderstanding and guilt. His death forced me to face once again who I am and what I have become through weakness, brokenness and love. Have I really learned to embrace suffering as I have learned to embrace love? Have I learned that sometimes there is no answer for why or why me? Have I learned that relationships with God, my friends and family are something that I should never take for granted?

I have seen rejection and it has an evil face. I have experienced pain and it has ushered me into brokenness. I have touched love and it has introduced me to grace. I have felt God's strength and marveled at it in my weakness. All of these things have led me to God where I have found solace, peace and forgiveness in the person of Jesus Christ. It is in Him that I have found my way and discovered who I am and where I am going in life. It is God that I will trust with my life today as I wave a happy and sad goodbye to yesterday and look forward to tomorrow.

I have known love and lost it. I have loved again deeply and have been very blessed. I have walked the same way as many before me and I have survived and thrived. Scripture tells us, just as God in his mercy is the God of all comfort, we are to comfort others.

Blessed be the God and Father of our Lord Jesus Christ, the Father of mercies and God of all comfort, who comforts us in all our affliction so that we will be able to comfort those who are in any affliction with the comfort with which we ourselves are comforted by God.
2 Corinthians 1:3-4 (NASB)

My Spur friends helped me in the process of healing. The Spurs were available to comfort, love, listen and sustain me as we walked toward Jesus together in our brokenness. I do not have to walk through life in the grip of fear and discouragement. God's arms are holding me in the present, and with a smile I confidently wave a silent hello to the future.

Strength and dignity are her clothing and she smiles at the future.
      Proverbs 31:25 (NASB)

A Time to Show Up
Exchanging Rings
by Kathleen Page Clark

....He has sent Me to heal the brokenhearted.....
Luke 4:18 (NKJV)

*R*eality was nearing. The court date was set and that dreaded date was approaching quickly. To my surprise, I was able to "choose" the court date once I was told all the paper work was ready and the holidays were over. Why not January 24? Two years earlier, my mother had died on that day, so why not commemorate two deaths on that day—the death of my mother and the death of a twenty-two year marriage.

I was careful to give that day a lot of thought. After all, the celebration of the marriage twenty-two years earlier had taken a lot of preparation, so I made sure that adequate preparations were made for this dreadful day.

I was told that I did not have to show up in court when the divorce was finalized, but I wanted to. I needed to face the reality and get some sort of healing closure. As we both stood before the judge, there was a long silence as he looked through the pages and pages of the settlement. I remember being disappointed that the judge was more interested in the division of our cars (eight for him and two for me) than he was with the obvious sadness in my eyes.

Before going to the courthouse, I had put on a new James Avery gold Celtic cross. My soon-to-be former spouse used to wear one like it in silver. Very soon we would no longer be wearing our hand-made and hand-hammered gold wedding rings, but the cross was my reminder that even though we were no longer man and wife, we were still Christians. My prayer and hope was that we could live out our separate lives treating each other as Christians. It has helped and been a real blessing to me.

As we walked out of the courtroom, I went over to my now former spouse, spread open my arms, gave him a hug and said "Peace be with you." That was not planned but felt spontaneously appropriate.

From the courthouse, I drove straight to the airport to pick up my younger sister, Martha, a Presbyterian minister. She was a senior pastor at the time and I asked her to fly in and do some sort of a divorce ceremony. I had put my rings on in church in the presence of God, my family and friends on my wedding day. I wanted to take this well-worn, almost smooth gold band with beautiful braided guard rings off in church in the presence of God and my family and friends on the day of my divorce. A wedding ring is a symbol that you are "taken" or "his." I knew that to go from wearing a wedding ring to a bare finger would be hard, so I bought a gold ichthus (fish) ring to wear. I needed something to visibly and emotionally remind me that I was still "taken" and "His"—the daughter of a King, my Lord and Savior, Jesus Christ. It worked!

Martha and I drove to the church at the designated time. The Spurs showed up as always! After memorable hugs, we gathered around the church altar and had the most beautiful, intimate and meaningful ceremony. My sister had me remove my rings; she blessed them into retirement and then blessed and put on the special one that I had bought. We had prayers for the healing of my heart, for my future as a single Christian woman and for the children. It was just what I needed.

The Spurs, as a group or as individuals, have a history of showing up in hard times and joyful times. All of the Spurs were not able to be there on that day. Who was there represented all those who were not. I was grateful for those who were able to be there. Their presence was important to me. It was the first day of the rest of my new life.

Kathleen retires her wedding rings
and puts on an ichthus (fish) ring to remind her whose she is.

A Time to Heal
by Sandra Talkington

Create in me a clean heart, O God,
and renew a steadfast spirit within me.
Do not cast me from your presence or take your Holy Spirit
from me. Restore to me the joy of your salvation and grant me a
willing spirit, to sustain me.
Psalm 51:10-12

A wave of guilt came over me early one morning as I lay in bed. My mind was going back to my father's last days. Only God could convict me of what I had done twenty-five years before. Tears started rolling down my cheeks as I realized the injustice to both my mother and my dad.

My parents had divorced after thirty-three years of marriage. In the summer of 1978, almost a year after our Spurs had its beginning, I was taking my children out to see my dad and then we would go to see my mother before school started.

When we arrived at Daddy's, he was in bed, which was very unusual for him. He was not feeling well at all. He was having pain down his right arm, which sounded like heart trouble to me. I took him to have tests the next day, leaving my children with my stepmother. He got a clean bill of health on his heart. However, shortly after we returned home, he received a call that would devastate us all. He had a spot on his lung. It was lung cancer, a very fast-growing kind. The doctors gave him two months to live, which sent us all into deep grief.

My brother and I spent lots of time with Daddy in the next two months, but the time went by too quickly.

As Daddy was dying, nearing the end of the two months, he asked to see Mother. Theirs had not been an amiable divorce. Mulling over the possible scenarios, I did not think it was a good idea. I was afraid of a confrontation between my mother and my stepmother, if she came. I never asked Mother to come to see him as he had wished.

About twenty-five years later, I lay in bed one morning knowing that the decision really had not been mine to make. Daddy had asked to see her and I should have honored his request.

During those years, I thought that I had told her that Daddy had wanted to see her when he was dying, but I did not make it happen. I did not feel any guilt about it until now. Suddenly I did. I knew then that I had to ask my mother for her forgiveness. That would be a very difficult thing to do, not knowing how she would respond.

The next morning I went over to see my mother. We were sitting out on the patio. I said, "Mother, I have something I need to talk to you about." She waited patiently while I related what had happened so many years ago. After I told her that I was wrong and feeling guilty not to have told her at the time that he wanted to see her, she said, "I always thought he wanted to ask me to forgive him." I replied, "I think he did, too."

There was healing in that moment. I am grateful God nudged me to do what I should have done long ago. God truly is the Great Physician and both my mother and I needed that healing!

The Spurs, my sisters in Christ, had helped me so much in coping with my parents' divorce. It was comforting to know that these dear friends with whom I shared my story would pray for me and the situation. Through their support and encouragement in Christ through the years, I have learned to listen when God speaks to me.

I am rejoicing in the healing of the relationship with my mother and in the joy and refreshment that comes with God's awesome cleansing power.

Left to right: Three generations in 2007. Grandson Brooks, grandmother Jewell Adams, granddaughter Grace and daughter Sandra Talkington.

A Time to Overcome Rage

by Carol Williams

In my distress I prayed to the LORD,
and the LORD answered me and set me free.
Psalm 118:5 (NLT)

Approximately twenty years ago, my dear hubby said, "Honey, I don't know what's going on but you're angry with me, the kids, God, life, everything and everybody! Why don't you talk to someone and see if you can get it all sorted out?"

Therefore, I began some chats with a Spur, Pat Reynolds, and some long-repressed feeling of six-year-old Carol began surfacing: *God, where are you when I need you the most? Why did you zap me with polio at age six and sister Sue escaped it all? At only six-years-old, how **bad** had I been to deserve that?*

I began to be aware of difficulties with trust and of a severe need to be "in control." Then, I might have said, "I love the Lord, but....." I became aware of a "deep beef" with God in my soul. A mental picture I had was that of reaching for God's hand to find bread and getting hold of a snake. I knew the scriptures presented a God worthy of trust, but my emotions revealed deep anxiety about trusting God.

At this time, Pat invited me to attend a Spur meeting. She assured me that these ladies were strong, growing Christians who, like me, were married to professionals in leading areas such as doctors, lawyers and businessmen. My husband, Jimmy, had risen in leadership with Campus Crusade for Christ and had then founded in 1973, Probe Ministries. I needed a safe place to "spill my beans"—a place where there was freedom to be open and honest and yet had true confidentiality.

The Spur "girls" could not have been more dear, accepting and non-judgmental. I cried, I raged and I was argumentative with any usual Christian answers, but patience with me was there.

I soon began to realize that these ladies had been through everything—teenagers on drugs and full of rebellion, grief over the loss of their spouse in death—all kinds of pain.

I realized it was all right to be totally honest with God about feelings and that He did not topple off of His throne with my accusations. Slowly, I sorted out some wrong theology and saw that a lot of my resentment toward God was misplaced. Since parents represent God in the life of a child, I saw that my long hospitalization with polio (for thirteen months, one thousand miles away from parents) caused deep feelings of abandonment and rage. All of this I had placed on my Lord. Slowly, with the Spurs' help, I came to see that God doesn't "zap" us, but rather, we live in a fallen world with polio germs, weeds, molesters, etc. Sometimes our Father shelters us from calamity, but other times, for reasons known only to Him, He allows us to be tested. Although I had accepted Christ as my Savior at age fourteen, I finally began to deeply trust and deeply **love** Him.

A Christian simply cannot have the peaceful life promised unless we learn to deeply trust God's goodness. When difficult things happen to us, they are allowed by a good, loving God who has our best interest in mind. Troubles and pain of all type—physical, emotional and spiritual—awaken us to God's Truth. With emotions healed and theology corrected and reassessed, there is a place of peace.

I am now seventy-two (2010) and am in a wheelchair permanently (post-polio syndrome). I still love to travel and I live life with zest. I experience joy daily. When I gather for Christmas with the Spurs, I sit at the beautiful grand piano at Mary Jo's home and play my heart out. We all sing the old familiar Christmas Carols. I sing praises and worship the Lord with gusto!

Carol Williams playing Christmas Carols

Spurred by Grace
Chapter Six

A Time for Encouragement

A Time to Trust   by Clarice Townes Miller
A Time to be Loved   by Barbara Clarkin
A Time to Rejoice   by Clarice Townes Miller
A Time to Live a Song   by Harriet Wallace

A Time to Trust
Our Relentless Journey
by Clarice Townes Miller

*Trust in the LORD with all your heart and
lean not on your own understanding:
in all your ways acknowledge Him and
He will make your paths straight.
Proverbs 3:5-6*

My friend, Carolyn Boyd, called and invited me to meet with a group of ladies from Dallas/Fort Worth. My life was so full that I could hardly say grace over it all but I felt the need for some new friends. Little did I know what was right around the corner for me!

Our family had moved to Denton, Texas, the year before and what a year it had been! Our oldest son was entering fourth grade; the four-year-old twin boys were enrolled in speech therapy and our three-year-old daughter had found a good friend across the street. My life was beginning to settle down and we were in the process of building a new home in Denton.

Another year had passed. Our twin boys were now in kindergarten. They had had a language all their own from the age of two. Their younger sister had been able to speak both their language and ours for several years. When we moved to Denton I was thrilled to find an excellent speech therapy program. After kindergarten, I took them to Dallas to be tested by a child psychologist who told me that they had visual perception and auditory memory problems. As a teacher, I knew that it involved a great deal of extra help beyond the regular classroom. We held them back a year. They continued with their speech and swimming therapy. We enrolled them in a private kindergarten/first grade class. At the end of that year a speech therapist and learning difference expert gave us very explicit recommendations of what they needed in order to go to public school. Her outlook for the success of the twins was very guarded, at best. They would need tutoring after school, several days a week. She gave me the name of the person that she felt was the best qualified in Denton. I called her and she became their tutor and second mother for the next seven years! Little did either of us know what was in store for us.

It was at this point that Carolyn called me. Several of us had met while our husbands were OB/GYN residents at Parkland Hospital in Dallas, Texas. My new friends, the Spurs, began a long, prayerful journey with me.

The Spurs were there for me when I heard the discouraging words from an expert that our sons might not graduate from high school. I was determined to get them all the help we possibly could! I had a new group of friends to be supportive and a tutor who was very helpful.

The time came when the twins were going to enter public school. I spent six months interviewing principals using the criteria of the expert. I explained to each principal what the "expert" recommended. After months, we selected the school that met most of the criteria of the specialist. I went to talk to that principal again to let him know that we hoped to enroll our two boys and their younger sister in the fall. He told me that I would have to wait until later to learn whether the children would be accepted in that school. The day school started, neither the boys nor their younger sister were enrolled anywhere. Their tutor, who had worked in the Denton school system, my husband and I went to the Superintendent of Schools to explain our dilemma. He immediately got them enrolled into that school. I was exhausted— physically, mentally and emotionally—after fighting with an institution that I thought was there to serve the needs of children! It was the first of many valuable lessons I would learn through the years. Thankfully, I had my Spur friends.

The children stayed in that school for a year until the end of the first six weeks of their second year. I went for a teacher's conference for one of the twins and his teacher told me she didn't believe that there was such a thing as a learning disability. It was a Friday afternoon and I didn't know what to do but I knew that our children could not stay in that school another day. With the help of their tutor, another friend and principal of another school we had our three children removed from one school and enrolled in another by Monday morning. The school was further away from our home and I had no guarantee that this would work. I felt like I was fighting an uphill battle, not knowing what the outcome would be!

Finally, our children were in a school where the boys were able to thrive; their tutor taught at that school; they were able to receive her help both during and after school. Now they were able to have a positive school experience.

Going from elementary school to junior high and then to high school was always a frightening and emotionally tense time for our family. It took several months of adjustments of their schedules and learning how to study for their classes until everyone settled back into a routine again. Thankfully, my Spurs prayed with me through moments of anxiety.

The boys were tutored through the seventh grade. Their tutor and I experienced multiple joys and disappointments. Sometimes, at my lowest point, I would say to the tutor that I was discouraged and wondered if all this extra work was worth it. She would boost my morale and encouraged me to continue our schedule that seemed never ending. She would sometimes say to me, "I think we need to take a break" and I would convince her that we had made so much progress that we couldn't stop. Many times, the boys would become discouraged and want to quit! For seven long years they would go three afternoons a week for an hour and a half after school to the tutor's home for extra help. All the while the boys were learning organizational skills, perseverance, tenacity, and how to compensate for their areas of weakness. By the time they reached high school their friends were asking about study habits; how to organize to write a term paper or how to study for a big exam! Not only did they make it to high school but they were also in several honors classes.

They both graduated from high school with a high B average with just tenths of a degree difference in their grade point average. My Spur friends were there to celebrate the victory of their high school graduation.

Our boys looked at several universities and colleges before deciding to go to a state university in East Texas. When my husband and the boys went to talk to one of the university advisers, he was discouraging when he found out that they had learning differences. He said he wasn't at all sure they were college material. Our sons knew that he would be proven wrong! They did very well; both graduated with a degree in finance and one was in an honorary scholastic fraternity.

God used both of these boys through the years to tell their story of how difficult it is to live with learning differences. Our family did a program for the Association of Children with Learning Differences in Denton to explain how this affects the whole family. While they were in college the twins, their tutor and I presented a program to the Texas Association of Children with Learning Differences telling their story of struggles, discouragements, accomplishments, times of despair, hope and joy. Later they presented a program to the state association encouraging parents, students and teachers to NEVER GIVE UP!

After marriage, one of the twins has been successful in the business world. He is now the President of a company. The other became a Christian Educator in the Presbyterian Church (U.S.A.). He received a Master of Christian Education from the Presbyterian School of Christian Education in Richmond, Virginia. After several years, he decided to go to seminary for a second Masters. He received a Master of Divinity degree from Louisville Presbyterian Seminary in Louisville, Kentucky.

Several years ago the three of us went to a private school in Florida to tell our story. We wanted to encourage both the teacher starting the program and the parents of the children enrolled.

The next day the twins told the students their story and how to persevere through painful times.

I think back through the years of the struggles, difficulties, hard work and perseverance that it took for all of us to accomplish a goal that seemed unattainable in the beginning. I think of those who were so very encouraging to us and also of those who were equally discouraging. We realized that God had entrusted us with these children's lives for a reason. We believed that with His help, the encouragement of my Spur friends and the hard work of the boys that this story reached far beyond what we could have possibly imagined. We offered our small mustard seed of faith and watched through the years as more and more was accomplished. The story isn't finished yet.

I thank my Spur sisters for being with me along the journey to hold my hand, to cry with me, to encourage me in times of discouragement and to rejoice with me in the times of victory. It was through each of them that I could feel God's constant care and love. How grateful I am for Carolyn's invitation to come to her house so many years ago and for the lessons we have learned!

Left to right: Twins Bryant Miller and Andrew Miller at age 4.

Left to right: Andrew, Linda Riley, their tutor, and Bryant.

A Time to be Loved

by Barbara Clarkin

Ask, and it shall be given you; seek, and ye shall find;
knock, and it shall be opened unto you.
Matthew 7:7 (KJV)

At some point in almost everyone's life we realize that we are on a search and usually don't know quite what we are looking for on this journey. I came to this realization when I was in my early 40s. It actually came as quite a surprise as I was quite competent and content in all I endeavored to do. I had seven children, who were all very active, and a physician husband who was totally devoted to his medical practice. Not that he ignored the family, but he didn't have much time to manage household or family responsibilities so I inherited them. Thank goodness, I did not have to go out and earn the money to support us as well as he could. Nor would I have had the stamina to do all he was required to do either physically or emotionally.

As a wife and mother I knew that I had made the children my first priority, as I was basically a single mother raising them. I appreciated and loved my husband but we seemed to have somewhat grown apart over the years. Religion was also very important to me. I was a member and still am of the Roman Catholic Church. My husband was a non-practicing Jew and supportive of my desire to raise our children in my faith (which is also a tenet of his faith that the children are raised in the mother's faith). The children went to Catholic schools for part of their education and received the sacraments. However, my eldest son with his inquisi-tive mind was beginning to doubt some of the dogma of our reli-gion. He became very involved with "Young Life" and studying the Bible. This led to a personal relationship with the Lord. Now I have to admit, I never even thought of the Lord in that aspect, nor did I know much about the Bible. I did know my church his-tory and the catechism.

This son soon highly influenced his siblings as they witnessed a transformation of his character. Scripture was now being quoted frequently with them as they, too, began to attend Bible studies. His father would retreat to his study when such conversations started while I would just listen. At times I found that I had to actually defend particulars about our Catholicism. I soon realized that I was the odd man out and decided to do something about this matter.

At this time I enrolled in Bible courses at my church. They were just theme studies and I wanted a more comprehensive study. I heard of other studies that I thought might enable me to have more enlightened conversations with my children that were held at other churches or in homes. Bible Study Fellowship (BSF) was one of these studies but it was by invitation only to attend a guest day. At a dinner party I mentioned this to a friend after a discussion about the Spirit's influence in one's life. I had just finished a "Life in the Spirit" seminar at our church and was very excited about this issue and I was becoming very interested in a deepening prayer life. She invited me to attend BSF guest day with her at which time I signed up to become a member.

Bible Study Fellowship was my exposure to more than I could have imagined. I enjoyed the sharing luncheons once a month with my class. I knew that I would like to have a group of women who shared their faith experiences on a consistent basis. Where would I find one? I did not know, as BSF groups changed each year, so the idea of keeping the same people was not very feasible.

Sometime later, I also learned about my friend's share and prayer group called the Spurs. This group of women not only shared their experiences in their walk with the Lord but also prayed for each other and their families and friends. I boldly asked how I could become a part of this group and was told that new Spurs were asked when that person's name had been placed "on the heart of one or two members" by the Lord. That person usually needed a group like the Spurs and maybe the Spurs needed them. Upon learning this, I was not sure I would become a Spur but I was content with that explanation.

A year or so later, I encountered the worst tragedy in my life and still consider it to be so—my husband left me for another woman. We had been married almost thirty-seven years. In the midst of this immense struggle, my friend called one day and invited me to a Spur meeting. She said the Lord laid my name on her heart at different times recently as He had done with another Spur that I knew. They both knew they had to act on this. How could they know I was desperate for some nurturing? I then realized that this was another of God's plans for me. Naturally I accepted, although I did attend with some fear of the unknown, as I knew so few in the group.

I walked through the door of the hostess's home and into the arms of everyone there welcoming me. Before the day was over, I had told my story (which was very humbling for me to do), been cried with and prayed over. I heard the needs of others discussed and prayed over that day and realized that I was where I needed to be then and hopefully would be forever. The group had already been gathering a good many years before I joined them so I had a lot of relational work to do. That took about a year, and one pro- found trip to England with them, for me to be aware that "what I said there stayed there." I was in a very safe place with wonderful friends. It also took them that long to be comfortable with who I was but they hung in there and the barriers came tumbling down.

Everyone needs a group like the Spurs. We have laughingly said that you can't become a part of the group unless you have a colossal experience involving pain or humbling circumstances. We are all sisters with Christ despite our own religious prefer- ences. That has led me to a deepening awareness and appreci- ation of other religions. We bring varying backgrounds to the table of the Lord and share our commonality with Him and each other. We have 'our' song, which is titled, "How Good and How Pleasant." The abiding refrain is, 'together in unity.'

The Lord has continued to bless me in other ways. A longtime acquaintance at my church became a widower and we began seeing each other. Neither of us planned another marriage but God had other ideas. Our families are delighted and so are we. Both of us have our Lord at the center of our lives, then with each other.

Though the Spurs no longer meet as frequently, when we do there is much laughing, some weeping, much celebrating of each other's blessings and lots of praying. We rarely take trips, as our lives are so busy as grandparents, caregivers, widows and retirees. I do not attend as often due to constrictions with a busy schedule. I do still pray for all of them and their families. They are always on my heart and I miss the days when we met more frequently. When I am with them, I am comforted by their presence. I thank the Lord for the blessing of the Spurs in my life. I also know that the search for life's meaning is ongoing, starting with a daily request to know the Lord's plan for that day only. I do know this, when I stumble, I know where I can reach up for hands to pull me up and pray with me—my faithful Spurs.

A Time to Rejoice
Celebration after Pain
by Clarice Townes Miller

LORD, you have assigned me my portion and my cup;
You have made my lot secure.
The boundary lines have fallen for me in pleasant places;
surely I have a delightful inheritance.
I will praise the LORD, who counsels me;
even at night my heart instructs me.
I have set the LORD always before me.
Because he is at my right hand, I will not be shaken.
Psalm 16:5-8

Memories came washing over me as I glanced at the adorable baseball hats neatly lined up at the bottom of Jennifer's bed! What these hats represented to Jennifer and me were the years of love, laughter, prayers and deep friendships between us and a precious group of soul sisters, named the Spurs.

A year earlier, our daughter, Jennifer, had moved from Houston, Texas, to Chattanooga, Tennessee. She had been working in corporate America and now was headed for a very different work environment. She was hired as the Program Director of Camp DeSoto, a Christian girls' camp in Mentone, Alabama. After her first summer of work, she came home for a week of rest and relaxation. While she was here she asked her dad, a physician, to feel a lump she had discovered under her collarbone. She could feel it only when she laughed hard. He said it was a swollen lymph node and if it didn't go away in a few weeks to see a doctor. Since she had just moved, she didn't have one and certainly didn't want to have to find one!

A few weeks later, the lump was still there. She called a family physician whose office was at the foot of Lookout Mountain, a few miles from camp. After examining her, he told her he wanted to run some tests. He called her telling her to find a general surgeon quickly. The physician called to tell us he believed that Jennifer had Hodgkin's' Disease. We were shocked! She was the picture of health—how could she be sick? She had been healthy all of her life. We could hardly believe his words. Within a week, I flew to Alabama to be with her while she had a biopsy. The news wasn't good. The surgeon told us that we needed to find an oncologist immediately.

Nothing about this made sense to us. She was our youngest child and had never been sick. How could she possibly have any-thing serious enough to need an oncologist?

She had lived in Houston within a few miles of M. D. Anderson Hospital, the prominent cancer center, less than a year before. Now she was in the middle of rural Alabama. Where could she get the help she needed? We had to find an oncologist in Alabama that accepted her medical insurance.

My husband remembered that he'd had a classmate in med-ical school that lived in Birmingham, Alabama. Our friend knew a local oncologist who he thought would be quite helpful.

In less than two weeks she had seen the first doctor, had a biopsy and was sitting in the oncologist's office. We waited ner-vously to be called back to his office. After blood work and waiting for a few minutes in the exam room, in walked a young, energetic doctor. Lots of questions were asked. Before treatment could begin he needed a bone marrow sample from her hip. He asked me to leave the room so that the procedure could be done. I told him that I wanted to stay with Jennifer to hold her hand. I knew how painful this was going to be. I didn't want to leave her alone and he let me stay. Within minutes he had done what he needed to do to know how to begin treatment. We also discovered during those many months of going back and forth to his office that just a few years before he had undergone this same treatment Jennifer was about to have! How ironic! He was certainly able to be more empathetic with her. He and his nurse knew just how to treat Jennifer—not only physically but emotionally, too. She was one of the youngest patients they had during those months of her treatment. She was informed she had cancer near her thirty-first birthday—hardly the gift she was expecting!

We had many decisions to make. We got busy making plans! After her Thursday treatments, someone would drive her from Birmingham to a vacant house at camp to hibernate four days until she recovered enough to be able to go to work on Monday. Camp owned a home that we used as her home-away-from-home for those next seven months. Four days after the treatment, she felt well enough to go back to her home in Chattanooga. This served several good purposes. First, she was away from her home during those few days when she felt so miserable and she didn't have to associate her home with those worst days. Second, a friend, a relative, or her dad and I would have a place to stay when we were helping her through those days after treatment.

Many relatives and friends called to offer their help. We were amazed and so grateful! Friends and family came from St. Louis, Missouri; Houston, Denton and Dallas, Texas; Memphis, Tennessee; Carthage and Oxford, Mississippi and Atlanta, Georgia. One of the Spurs came from Dallas to spend a weekend with her. What acts of love they performed during those days with her when she was so sick! What a sense of community love she felt!

In January, she couldn't stand her hair falling out. Her dear friend, Marsha, shaved her head. February, March and April were difficult months. I went to live at the Bibb House that was owned by Camp DeSoto to be close to Jennifer.

My Spur friends had decided they wanted a camp experience and also wanted to help Jennifer celebrate the end of her treatments. The week after Jennifer's last treatment, thirteen of my dear Spur friends drove from the Dallas/Fort Worth, Texas area to Mentone, Alabama for a four day camp experience. As a surprise they each brought Jennifer thirteen adorable hats to celebrate the end of her treatments (and to cover her head!).

There are no words to describe the celebration that we had together—laughter, joy, tears, happiness that only those who have walked through the valley can imagine! These friends joined arms around her to lift her up and together we all thanked God for being at her right hand so that she would not be shaken!

Jennifer gave each of her friends who came to stay with her a small gift after her treatments were over. I kept this note that she wrote friends and family:

In December 2000 I was reading through the Psalms and was struck by Psalm 16. It seemed to address all my fears and issues about my cancer—but more importantly about my life. God's sovereignty covers all of life's joy and pain. I wanted to give to you, the people who shared my treatments with me, a small gift and encourage you with the words that spoke to me so powerfully this year. Use this journal to record your journey with God—struggles and blessings! Words will never be able to express my love and gratitude for your love, care and friendship! Love, Jennifer

It has now been over twelve years since Jennifer's story was finished and to this day she continues to get a clean bill of health from her doctor.

Thanks to God and to our many good friends who held our hearts through the pain!

Jennifer Miller, holding the hats the Spurs gave her to wear after her hair loss from chemo. Camp DeSoto, Meltone, Alabama. 2001

A Time to Live a Song
"Blest be the Tie that Binds"
Written by John Fawcett in 1782

by Harriet Wallace

I will praise the name of God with a song;
I will magnify him with thanksgiving.
Psalm 69:30 (ESV)

The words to "Blest be the Tie that Binds" song sum up our relationships with each other as Spurs. It succinctly describes who and what we are all about. Here are the words:

Blest be the tie that binds
Our hearts in Christian love
The fellowship of kindred minds
Is like to that above.

Before our Father's throne
We pour our ardent prayers
Our fears, our hopes, our aims are one
Our comforts and our cares.

When for a while we part
This thought will soothe our pain
That we shall still be joined in heart
And hope to meet again.

From sorrow, toil and pain
And sin we shall be free
And perfect love and friendship reign
Through all eternity.

The story behind this song is a wonderful one and gives special meaning to it.

> Dr. John Fawcett was an ordained Baptist minister. He accepted a call to pastor a small and impoverished congregation at Wainsgate in Northern England. After spending several years at Wainsgate, he received a call in 1772 to succeed Dr. Gill to minister to a large and influential Baptist church in London. He accepted the call and preached his farewell sermon. The wagons were loaded with his books and furniture, and all was ready for the departure, when his parishioners gathered around him, and with tears in their eyes begged of him to stay. His wife said, "Oh John, John, I cannot bear this." "Neither can I," exclaimed the good pastor, "and we will not go. Unload the wagons and put everything as it was before." His decision was hailed with great joy by his people. They stayed at Wainsgate and unpacked their bags. He wrote this poem that later became a hymn in commemoration of the event. (Information taken from multiple sources.)

I have often thought of what else Dr. Fawcett might have shared with his parishioners after writing this poem. In my imagination, these are my thoughts of what he might have said that could apply to the Spurs as well:

> *Blest be God our Father. It is He who has brought us together and bound our hearts as one in His love. We are one because He lives in each one of us. We are one because we have the mind of Christ, each being unique just as the Father, Son and Holy Spirit are unique yet One. We have been together these many years, sharing our lives through fellowship, worship*

and prayer. We have bared our souls in prayer, and shared a vision of being burden bearers to one another. Whether we are together or apart, we are with each other in spirit. This tie that binds us. This love. It cannot be explained.."

I then picture Dr. Fawcett holding up the cross and saying:

"Look upon the One who loved us like this."

Spurred by Grace
Chapter Seven

A Time for Restoration

A Time for a New Name

by Maureen Eagan

.......and you shall be called by a new name.....
Isaiah 62:2 (ESV)

The invitation came at a big crossroads in my life (sometimes called "midlife crisis")! Pat Reynolds invited me to attend a get-together in Fort Worth with a small group of women who originally knew each other because of their husbands' vocations.

Pat, who had grown up in Fort Worth, was a close friend with Carolyn Boyd, who was hosting that day's get-together. The group had really bonded during a small retreat that Pat had facilitated and wanted to keep meeting from time to time. Carolyn's home was spacious, very warm and beautifully situated on a bluff. The views from her house included looking down at a golf green and across the pool and cabana looking into trees and tree tops—very much of a retreat setting. We were greeted with coffee and some of Carolyn's famous homemade breakfast goodies. Those same breakfast goodies have been a signature treat trailing us through many meetings in different places. The women were all warm, attractive, outgoing and very relaxed with each other. There were probably around ten present and I felt equally comfortable just blending in and listening to their exchanges of conversation about their daily life activities which some in the group shared.

Since it became such a significant day in my life, I remember vividly what I wore—pants and a silk shirt in a light sage green—very apropos for new growth!

Lunch was served in Carolyn's formal dining room in full celebration with her fine china, silver and crystal! I was impressed! No paper plates, napkins, lap trays, etc. She was celebrating her friendships with a feast!

After Carolyn's lunch, Pat gathered us together in a circle and asked us each to share one thing: How did we get our name and what do we feel about it? It turned out to be a much deeper question than it seemed as the women shared their history and feelings. Things started popping into my mind but I was still able to listen to the sharing and the insights shared by the women. When it came my turn, almost near the end, I shared that I had just found out from my mother that my father had named me Lois. Where did he get the name? He had gotten it from an old girlfriend! When I asked my mother if she had picked out a name for me, she said, "No!" That seemed strange to me, but my thoughts turned to the fact that I was born during the height of the depression and almost certainly had not been planned. Perhaps this was her way of denying an unwanted pregnancy.

Then I shared with the Spurs that when we moved after my third year in school, I asked mother if I could go by my middle name, Maureen, at the new school. She agreed! I loved using my middle name and my fourth grade year turned out to be my happiest grade school year. When we moved to Texas, I went back to using Lois as my handwriting teacher was furious with the way I made those "Yankee" r's!

Fast forward to the late 70s and 80s. I started to remember how much I liked being called Maureen. Woody, my husband, had business conferences in different cities in the states and eventually a yearly one in England. I asked him if he would mind registering me as his wife, Maureen! He agreed and for five days (or a week or so), I was known only as Maureen. Strange as it may sound, when someone spoke my name Maureen, I felt like everything in me responded!

After I finished sharing, Carolyn Boyd looked straight at me and in a no nonsense tone said "We are going to call you Maureen!" It felt like someone turned a key in me and unlocked the real person. I felt christened! I left that day knowing something very freeing: My new name released my true identity!

Maureen Eagan holding her "decade change" album that many Spurs also received.

A Time for Insights
Insights along the Way
by Clarice Townes Miller

"Come to me, all you who are weary and burdened,
and I will give you rest...for I am gentle and humble
and you will find rest for your souls."
Matthew 11:28-29

The Spurs had been meeting for a couple of years. We decided it would be fun and helpful if we went to Colorado for a retreat. I was still beginning to get to know everyone. At times I felt very different and isolated from the group. Many lived in the same community, were part of the same social clubs or church and I wondered if my being part of this group was of importance to them or to me. I didn't feel this often, but there were times I wondered. I felt that some were much more spiritual than I and had their lives more together than mine. They seemed to have answers to life's perplexing questions and I was struggling with many. They knew my superficial self, but they didn't really know me. For that matter, neither did I!

I was born into a prominent Christian family in a small Mississippi town. I was the oldest of four children and took that role seriously—having all the characteristics that entails. The 1940s and 1950s shaped my internal and external life. For the most part, my life was idyllic. While this was true for me and my siblings, our parents were dealing with difficult family issues. Our mother's oldest brother was an alcoholic who caused the family great heartache. As I became older we learned her sister suffered from depression. I was a very young child during WWII but I was protected from all that pain. There were numerous other painful secrets that I didn't learn until I was an adult. As is often the case in the Deep South, the pain and suffering of life is glossed over and folks greet each other with smiles. One's world could be crumbling but it's not shared or spoken of. I learned early to not ask questions, to mask my real feelings, to believe that those in authority were always right and to roll along with life making the best of whatever came my way. I learned to keep family secrets.

I married as soon as I graduated from college. My husband took over Daddy's role of protector and provider. I was sheltered throughout my younger life so I wasn't taught many life skills. I didn't learn to balance a checkbook until after I was married.

By the time the Spurs went on the Colorado trip my idyllic world was beginning to crumble. I had more questions than answers about my life as a wife, mother, sister, friend—and disciple of Christ. Even though I had a happy marriage, my OB/GYN husband was gone more than he was home; we were struggling to have weekend getaways so that we could finish a conversation. We had just learned that our six-year-old twins had severe learning differences. I was struggling with being a good mother to these two plus not neglecting our older son or younger daughter. I was learning that school systems and principals often have their own agendas that didn't include caring for those with very specific needs. My youngest sister was in college about fifty miles away. I had promised our dad on his deathbed that I would care for her. She had bi-polar, alcohol and drug problems. We both were dealing with emotional pain because of Daddy's death.

She was fourteen years younger than I and more like our oldest child than a sibling. She often turned to my husband and me for emotional help. I was trying to care for her along with trying to shoulder my duties of wife and mother. I had been so focused on caring for all those around me that my internal world was spinning out of control. I was beginning to feel depressed, angry and totally out of control with all the balls I was juggling.

All I had wanted was to be a good wife and mother. It was the 1970s and I was feeling pressure to be more than a wife and mother. The message of the times was that women should be MORE—have a job, a career—something more than family. So, I was also struggling with that. However the other heart issues held far more importance for me. Why was it so difficult to get in touch with my feelings? Why couldn't I explain to my husband what I was struggling with? Why couldn't the school principal understand how much I wanted help for our children, but also for those children whose parents had less of a voice than I? I had a background in education and could have been resourceful to him if he had been open. I had to fight to be heard and then was turned down. I worried about our other two children feeling abandoned while my husband and I spent so much time helping our twins. I felt very vulnerable when I flew to Colorado to be with my Spur friends.

Pat, one of the Spurs, asked us one morning to draw a picture of how we saw ourselves. I took pen in hand and drew a picture, not realizing how revealing it would be to her (or to me!). My picture of my body was regular size, except for my legs and I drew them HUGE. Pat took one look at that picture and explained, "You feel that you have the weight of the world on you and you are trying to hold it all up!" I was speechless. Through that simple drawing I had revealed to another person what I was feeling internally. What a relief and sense of freedom it gave me for someone else to recognize that and help me get in touch with my inner core! God had used my friend to help me know why I was feeling the way I was. It was a major breakthrough for me. I was beginning to learn that I didn't have to keep everything bottled up within; that I could risk sharing with my friends what I was experiencing in life—the good, bad and ugly! I had spent the first thirty-plus years not sharing with myself or others who God had created me to be. I learned how very important it was to be real—open, honest and vulnerable—with myself and others.

A self-portrait drawn by Clarice Townes Miller.
Note size of legs!

It took many years for me to become comfortable sharing my pain, struggles, disappointments and failures. The process of sharing feelings and inner struggles has become easier through the love and encouragement of my Spur sisters. They have listened to my struggles with helping our twin boys, helping my sister with her problems, coping with my mother's rape and our daughter's scare with Lymphoma, and having little contact with one of our grown sons for a period of time.

As I've reflected about the importance of the Spurs, I've realized that we have helped one another accept whatever life throws at any one of us. They have walked beside me through the many years as we continued to find the helpful teachers and tutors for our twins. We have celebrated together when they reached important goals. Many years later, the Spurs were with me through another painful journey.

Our son and his second wife were married for seven years. The first three were happy for all of us as we got to know one another. Our daughter-in-law and I got along well and often shared long conversations and visits. She was a good stepmom to our granddaughter. Things gradually began to change. Small misunderstandings became huge, misinterpretations of events occurred and angry phone calls were made.

We tried numerous avenues to bridge the gap. Weeks grew into months—months into years. For four difficult years we prayed that there would be reconciliation between our son's family and us. We prayed that our granddaughter and her dad would spend quality time together again. We feared that our fragile relationship with our son was over. We rarely saw or talked to him.

I was once again facing a crisis with one of our children. There were major differences this time. Earlier our children were very young and totally dependent on us. Now, as parents, we were dealing with a crisis of a grown son. We felt he had to discover answers for himself. All we could do was wait, pray and hope that someday we would be reconciled.

I remembered the drawing I had made years earlier showing that I felt the weight of the world on my legs. If I drew a picture today it would be a picture of me kneeling in worship with my arms outstretched releasing this heartache to God. I have come full circle from that cold day in Colorado. Hopefully I'm wiser and can accept now that one only has control of his/her own life. The older I get the more I realize I'm most at peace when I relinquish that to God, too.

Even though, I had no idea how our relationship would work out, I have had an inner peace, calm and confidence that I didn't have when I was in my thirties and struggling with different matters. I'm now in my late sixties. We have had many more life experiences. I've learned

- to trust more the faithfulness of a loving God who never leaves or forsakes us
- to seek Jesus who walks beside us in our daily journey
- to be open to the Holy Spirit who dwells within each of us

- to depend on His guidance and encouragement
- to accept that God's ways and timing are not mine.

My Spur friends have been beside me loving, encouraging and supporting me. I have learned to share my feelings, to be honest and to realize that God often uses others to speak His truth.

After a long, troubling struggle, our son called one day telling us that he was divorcing his wife. We realized that he had been in pain and unrest for several years, even though we had not spoken to him. The destruction it was causing everyone had to end. Finally, he was free to be the father his daughter needed. We prayed our son's, his daughter's and our relationship would be restored. We have had to commit our thoughts, emotions and ways to the leading of the Holy Spirit. This is an ongoing process that takes time and healing.

Our children are in God's hands. I can love them, pray for and with them, but I must continue "to let them fly away" to become what God has in store for them. As much as I would love to protect them from life's difficulties, that isn't my job. Only God knows how to shape and mold their lives. Parents observe and rejoice at what God is able to do with their children's lives. Thankfully, I've had a group of loving women, called the Spurs, to walk beside me, listen to my cries of joy and pain and to see the results of prayers answered God's way.

A Time to Search
The Desperation of a Mother's Heart
by Sally Renshaw with Molly Dummit

What do you think?
If a man owns a hundred sheep, and one of them wanders away,
will he not leave the ninety-nine on the hills and
go to look for the one that wandered off?
And if he finds it, I tell you the truth,
he is happier about that one sheep than about
the ninety-nine that did not wander off.
In the same way your Father in heaven
is not willing that any of these little ones should be lost.
Matthew 18:12-14

My son, Scott Renshaw, was living in Naples, Florida. The last we knew he had been on a trip to New York and was quite ill when he returned to Florida. In fact, he had missed his grand-mother's funeral on January 3, 2000, because he was ill. Soon there was no communication and letters were returned with no return address. We knew of no friends to contact. I never felt he was in physical danger. There was only silence. He was shutting us out.

At several Spurs' meetings Scott was the focus of our prayers, asking God to protect him and for guidance to know what to do to find him. I felt the loving, constant prayers of the whole group. I was not alone, all of those mothers' hearts were crying out to God with me. Molly kept saying, "We will know what to do and when to do it. We will find him!" The waiting and listening is always hard, but we wanted God's direction. When we look back over how we were directed to the right time and right place, with every single moment working for our advantage, it is quite amazing.

Step by step this is the story:

Left to right: Sally Renshaw and Molly Dummit
start out on their adventure of a lifetime!

Molly received a phone call from a company promoting a travel group. We met in Dallas to listen to their promotion and received two vouchers for airplane tickets to Orlando, Florida. The vouchers had to be used within the year. Ten days before the year was up, we realized we had to go. One of the Spurs' daughters researched through her business and found two addresses that might be a possible answer to the search for Scott.

Molly and I could have just bought our tickets and planned this trip like we usually do, but we did not trust our timing or plans. God's timing and plans were perfect. He definitely walked before us, and we stepped in His footsteps all the way there and back. The whole group of Spurs was with us in prayer. One of the Spurs slipped some money and a very special devotional book in Molly's pocket before we left. The devotional book turned out to be our daily map. What a blessing!

Off we flew to Orlando. A little laughter and lightheartedness awaited us the first night we arrived. After we rented a car and drove to the "two nights free" motel, there were just a few hours left for a quick run through Disneyland. We parked the car in a huge parking lot and both checked the approximate spot on a specific aisle. The park closed at 11:00 p.m.. There we were searching for a car that we remembered only as navy blue and did not seem to be at the remembered location. I went to talk to the attendant for fear the car had been stolen. When I returned, most of the cars were gone, and there was Molly in the middle of the lighted parking lot laughing and talking on her cell phone. Her son, Jeff, back in Texas, had called to see if we were all right, and now he would not let us hang up until we found the car. A couple with children drove me around to try my key in several cars that were left. Yea! We found it and returned to the motel wondering if this were a foretaste of the searching trip ahead of us.

We left the next morning for Sebring, Florida, halfway to Naples. There, awaiting us, was a condo owned by another Spur, Molly's daughter, Elizabeth. She said we could stay as long as we wanted, but we stayed only one night.

Early afternoon the next day we drove into Naples and straight to our destination, a Spur's in-law's gorgeous home. Our hosts welcomed us and since they knew of our mission, we left immediately to check out the addresses we had. The first address was a gated community. We had to go into the office to get his apartment number and to know if he even lived there. The receptionist would not give out any information. I said to her, "I am his mother and have not heard from him in two years." The receptionist told us to wait outside for her. When she came out, she told us she could be fired for telling us, but she gave us Scott's apartment number and opened the gate for us. She did this because she had a brother missing for two years! God put the right people in our path every time and had the perfect place for us to stay every night.

We knocked on the door of the apartment several times. No answer—what to do next? We decided to wait on the Lord for directions. We sat in the car outside in front of Scott's apartment reading our devotional book. We looked up and a gentleman was coming out of a nearby apartment. He stopped and sat on his steps. By chance, would he know anything about Scott? We asked the man, named George, if he knew Scott Renshaw. He asked, "Scott from Texas?"

Scott is such an extremely private person, we were not surprised when he said, "I'm probably the only person he has visited in this apartment complex." There was God again going before us. George said he thought Scott had gone to Thailand. Then he mentioned that he thought Scott was separated from his wife and baby.

There was a long moment of silence! Molly and I dared not look at each other for fear of giving away our shock. George, our new friend, told us as much as he could and then drove us around the complex looking for Scott's car. His garage door was closed. It was getting late so George gave us his phone number and left just before dark.

From the facts obtained from a Spur's daughter, we had a phone number for Scott's wife, Mayra. We decided to call that very evening. We could hardly breathe, much less wait until morning to meet this little family. There was no answer so I left a message on the answering machine asking to meet them. The next day about noon, I received a call from Mayra, inviting us to come to her house at 3:00 p.m., after the baby, Olivia, was up from her nap.

When we arrived, Mayra was standing outside holding a darling little Renshaw (no way denying that). She was twenty months old and seemed to know immediately that this visit was something special. There was Mayra with dark, curly hair holding this little blonde baby, Olivia. Mayra's brother, Marco, and his wife, Jennie, as well as Ximena, Mayra's niece, were all there to meet us.

Mayra was loving and open with us and shared many details about Scott and his departure upon hearing of Mayra's pregnancy. How painful it was to imagine Mayra's delivery and the first few weeks afterward, but God had sent her many caring friends. There was nurse Betty who arranged for her to have a comforting experience in the hospital. Mayra resumed her job of cleaning houses much too soon after Olivia's arrival. I am not sure who helped with the baby in the beginning, but her niece, Ximena, soon came from Ecuador to be her nanny. We learned that Scott had returned when Olivia was six months old and wanted to help care for Olivia, who was by then taking chemotherapy for liver cancer every weekend for six months. Scott and Ximena did not get along and eventually, Mayra had to ask Scott to leave. Mayra had not heard from him since that time.

We visited with Mayra, baby Olivia, and Ximena a few more times, becoming better acquainted with them. We were mesmerized by Olivia and loved them all. On our last visit, Mayra insisted that we return. She was ecstatic that Olivia had loving grandparents as well as aunts, uncles, and cousins who wanted to know her. Scott was not found, but Olivia was. We had accomplished our mission. We knew Scott was safe and we had a new granddaughter. We wanted to be a big part of her life, emotionally and financially. God's amazing grace!

The Spurs were praying with me and encouraging our family with each return trip. What a blessing! Many visits later Mayra and the whole family planned a trip to Texas. The date was set and shortly before the planned visit, Scott called! This was the first we had talked to him in two years. What an indescribable joy! He told us he would be home on the day of Mayra's planned arrival. When Mayra heard the news, she cancelled the trip. She was not comfortable with the prospect of their being together at that time. She also felt that we needed time to heal our relationship with Scott.

Scott drove home and after our joyful reunion and dinner, he told us he had something to tell us. Before he could elaborate, I told him we had already met and visited with Mayra many times. He was amazed at all of the pictures we had of Olivia and her family taken on our many trips to Naples. I sensed a wave of relief washing over him.

As if anticipating his return, our rental house in Texas was empty and undergoing renovation. Scott enthusiastically participated in that work as well as other day-to-day chores around the farm. While he had made it clear from the beginning that his stay was temporary, it was unclear what might determine his departure. It was the tenuous relationship with Mayra. He eventually called her to explore the possibility of his talking with Olivia and becoming a part of her life. Mayra was agreeable whereupon Scott went to Naples to "test the water." He was pleasantly surprised at his acceptance by Mayra as far as Olivia was concerned. The next month he moved back to Naples so he could be near his daughter. There he remains today, as she is the focus of his life.

Sally Renshaw holding her new granddaughter, Olivia.

Sally Renshaw's son, Scott, holding his
daughter Olivia a few years later.

A Time to Confront

by Barbara Clarkin

A man who lacks judgment derides his neighbor,
but a man of understanding holds his tongue.
A gossip betrays a confidence, but a trustworthy
man keeps a secret.
Proverbs 11:12-13

*O*ne lovely Sunday morning after I had returned from church, I received a phone call from two of my Spur friends. They wanted to know if they could stop to chat for a few minutes. Of course, I was delighted. At the time I was single and company was almost always welcome—especially good friends.

I was a bit surprised that they had the time as it was on the weekend. In a short time the doorbell was ringing. I anticipated their visit with pleasure. After entering, I offered them a beverage but they declined as they said they did not have long to stay. I started some conversation but it was soon ended, as my friends were not engaging in it enthusiastically.

The intention of the visit was then revealed. They had come to speak about an issue of impropriety on my part. I was baffled and anxious as I sat listening to them. As an adult I was definitely being reprimanded and began to feel a little defensive. I also feared that perhaps I would be asked to leave the Spurs!

The offense on my part was not earth shattering. I had made a statement while at work I had heard from another Spur at one of our meetings. It was said in front of a person who happened to be a friend of several of the Spurs and she informed a couple of them later of this statement. At no time had names been mentioned but the fact that I had revealed a comment this person knew I would know nothing about unless it came from a Spur was of interest to her. She knew of our tell nothing outside of meeting rules and thought that these Spurs should be informed of the situation.

I mentioned that no harm was intended and that it was an innocent remark which could not endanger anyone's reputation. I also added that I did not mention the name of the Spur who made the remark. I apologized and asked what they wanted me to do to make retribution. It was agreed to say nothing more was best. I felt humbled and suggested resigning from the group. This was not what they wanted. They just felt that the incident needed to be addressed so that there would be no more such incidents. They also said they knew I had not intended harm to anyone but since the episode was one of gossip, a sin, it needed to be addressed.

Our Lord tells us in scripture that we need to confront sinners and should do it with more than one person. It is also to be done with love and mercy. My precious Spur friends did just that and I am forever grateful to them. We hugged and they left. When we can come before our friends or family with confidence in the truths we have been given by our Lord, we know that the relationship will not be shattered but grow stronger.

Most of the Spurs never knew of this incident until now, but I want others as well as the two of them to know what godly women make up this beloved group of Spurs. May we all follow our Lord as diligently.

A Time for Courage
Astounding Love
by Clarice Townes Miller

In all these things we are more than conquerors
through him who loved us. For I am convinced that
neither death nor life, neither angels nor demons,
neither the present nor the future, nor any powers,
neither height nor depth, nor anything else in all creations,
will be able to separate us from the love of God
that is in Christ Jesus our Lord.
Romans 8:37-38

*T*couldn't say the word—much less connect it with my mother! The most I could do was spell the word: R-A-P-E. A chill swept over my body. How could something so horrifying be true? Where does one turn after hearing such painful news?

It was July 10, 1982. I received a phone call from my brother telling me that I needed to come home to Mississippi as soon as possible. On that Sunday afternoon, my seventy-year-old mother, the first woman elder elected in the Presbyterian Church in a small southern town, had gone back to the church to be sure that one of the back doors of the church had been locked. As she turned the corner to leave, a young man met her in the education wing. She was knocked to the floor and raped!

Slowly she got up, walked out into the sunlight and as she was locking the door, thankfully, a couple from the church was driving by. She waved them down, told them what had happened and they took her to the emergency room at the hospital.

She was badly bruised and scarred by the emotional and physical trauma that had happened. As I listened to my brother telling me this, I felt I was in a dream. Certainly I wasn't hearing this tale about OUR mother who was such a saintly, gracious, southern lady who demonstrated her Christian faith daily. How could this possibly be true? What could I possibly do or say to her that could bring her comfort or healing? How could she go on with her life in a normal way? More and more questions came rushing and yet I had no answers.

The next day three of our four children and I left to be with her for the next two weeks. There was little to do or say except to be with her. There was healing that came to both of us by just being together. The words that I worried about saying weren't necessary. It was just being with her that mattered. It reminded me of how often God reminds us that He wants to just be in our midst wherever we are, whatever we are experiencing in this life. So, I remained for those two weeks caring for her.

We learned that there were several other ladies raped that day and Mother was the only one who was willing to go to court to testify. When I think of that I marvel because it was only by God's grace that was possible. Mother was a quiet, introverted lady and the last thing she would have wanted to do was to tell that story in a courtroom.

Mother knew that was the right thing to do! By doing this, it also prolonged the length of time that it took for her to get past this event. God always provides the strength and courage that we need, regardless of the circumstances.

As soon as I returned home from my visit with Mother, I called and asked the Spurs to meet. I needed their prayers and presence with me to keep me from falling. My faith had been badly shaken by this horrible crime to one that I loved so much. I had no answers to my many questions!

Five months later we were home for the Christmas holidays and she got a phone call from her attorney asking her to come give a deposition. I was thankful that I was there so I could go with her.

In February there was a trial and she didn't want any of her four children to be there. My sister came and stayed home to be with her after the hearing. My brother who lived in town sat outside the courtroom while she was testifying. We each wanted to be there to support her, but she said that remembering her in our prayers would be more helpful to her than being there. She felt it would make it more difficult to tell the story in court if we were there. So we honored her wishes.

After the trial Mother wrote a letter telling us about the court procedures. In this letter she writes telling what it was like as she sat in the witness chair:

"During the whole time I was very aware of the Presence of the Holy Spirit. I know that the prayers of my family and church worked in a mysterious way to enable me to be and do things I could not possibly have done in my own strength. My voice did not fail and I was in control of my emotions at all times. When the other lawyer questioned me, it was rough, as I knew it would be, but I did not falter. I say this because I know that it was not my own strength but His.

"There were three possible verdicts—guilty of rape, guilty of attempted rape (a much less severe penalty) or not guilty. The jury was out for thirty-five minutes and brought back a verdict guilty of rape. Later Judge Morgan gave the sentence for twenty-five years, which was the highest penalty. He would be eligible for parole review in ten years.

"As painful as all of this has been I feel I have learned some things from it. I know that I have come to know my Lord and Savior in a deeper way. I have experienced His love and care. His faithfulness— the way He always fulfills what

He promises in His Word. I already knew this, but all of this has increased my faith and my faithfulness."

As I've written this and reread the letter Mother sent us after the trial, I'm very aware that one of the reasons that I need to share this story is so that we can be reminded of the deep faith of our mother who died in 1984. I also feel that in retelling this story other family members who come after her—her grandchildren and great-grandchildren—will know and hear the words of a very committed, faithful follower of Christ. I believe that by sharing these stories of how God has worked in our lives that others will come to know Him in a deeper way.

A part of me does not want to share this story. As I've wrestled with this, I've become more convinced that I should. Many terrible things happen in life to innocent people—fine outstanding Christians—and we ask, "Why?" Some of us lash out at God, become angry, depressed and turn away from our faith, family and church. As I've reflected and wrestled with this, I've realized that there will not be answers to that one and many other questions. So we are left to decide how we'll use the pain. Perhaps, as we share the stories we are able to help others who are also fellow strugglers. So often we, who call ourselves Christians, only share our stories of victory. It is seldom that we share our struggles that give us no answers. Through sharing this painful story, I hope that you will find hope and peace through your pain.

Webster's dictionary defines the word courage as the attitude of facing and dealing with anything recognized as dangerous, difficult or painful, instead of withdrawing from it.

I pray that those who read this will understand what courage is in today's world. It is making the difficult decision to:

- take a stand alone, with God's help
- do the right thing even when it seems impossible
- speak the truth

- be willing for the Potter to take the brokenness and ugliness of life and make it into a beautiful, serviceable pitcher to splash God's healing power and strength to all those willing to be open to His love.

Through those many months of hurting, wondering, questioning and waiting, my Spur friends held me, cried with me, prayed for and with me for healing as we walked through a very dark time in my family's life. Not only was my mother's faith strengthened through this time—mine and the Spurs were also. Thank you, God, for always being present with us in our darkest hours of pain!

Clarice Townes Miller's mother, Adelaide Horton Townes, holding her youngest grandchild, Jonathan Michael Mansfield (5 months old).

A Time For Reconciliation

by Molly Dummit

*All this is from God, who reconciled us to himself through Christ
and gave us the ministry of reconciliation.
2 Corinthians 5:18*

*D*ivorce is everywhere—it's everywhere!
The Spurs have not been spared!
When one of our children marries, we immediately try to adopt
their spouses into our family as our own. We learn to love that
child as one of our children.

Who can turn love on and off? Not I! Neither can many of the
Spurs who have experienced their son's and daughter's divorces.

My son and his wife, Elizabeth, were married several years
before they had a child, a special little boy. They decided to
divorce when the child was only three. My husband and I were
brokenhearted. We loved each of them deeply and we prayed for
all three to be protected and given new happy lives. This eventually happened. My former daughter-in-law married one of my
best Spur friend's son!

At the Mother-Daughter dinner, Elizabeth, my former
daughter-in-law, sat between Phyllis, her new mother-in-law, and
me. Elizabeth stood up and introduced both of us as her mothers.
It was quite a testimony to others experiencing the same thing
and a lovely picture of reconciliation.

Molly Dummit *(left)* and Phyllis White *(right)* share Elizabeth *(center)* at the Mother-Daughter dinner.

A Time to be Restored

by Maureen Eagan

I will restore to you the years the locusts have eaten......
You shall know that I am in the midst of Israel, and that I,
the LORD, am your God and there is none else.
And my people shall never again be put to shame.
Joel 2:25,27 (ESV)

At my first meeting with the Spurs, I was in a state of deep dissatisfaction and discouragement. I was currently serving as president of the Women of the Church and found myself once again in the grip of the "shoulds" and "alien" expressions of one's spiritual walk. I had somewhat of a "spiritual reputation" in our church, after being a Circle Bible moderator, a circle chairperson, Personal Faith and Family Life Chairman—all jobs in which I was fairly comfortable. I was asked to be president of the Women of the Church two times. After first refusing, I felt the Lord was definitely nudging me to say, "Yes." My spiritual history had really begun when I made the crossover from being a "church goer" to having a life-changing experience with God watching Billy Graham on television.

Not having been raised in the church, I had no traditional background to stand on, but my life with Christ was real. His Word was changing me all the time and I think it must have showed in my interaction with the Women of the Church as they had repeatedly asked me to serve in different positions.

When I became president, I was told that the board meetings were always conducted using *Roberts Rules of Order*. "This is the way things should be done; this is the way you should believe: these are the things you should do." Where is the Holy Spirit in all that? No one talked about Jesus or the leading of the Holy Spirit but you heard a lot of things that translated into Duty and Order. I see now that the growing resistance and anger I felt went a lot deeper than the expectations of the Women of the Church.

I was raised pretty much by a single parent, my mother. My father was home about five percent of the time as he traveled; except for two brief years, he almost did not live with us. My mother grew up in a family situation that produced shame and anger that could easily turn to rage. She was driven to "be somebody" and that set her standard for mothering. Her Germanic heritage pushed her constantly with unrealistic and rigid expectations, and she constantly applied them to me as the only child. Perhaps I could become her dream! When I made an A in school, no praise followed. Her comment would be "next time make it an A plus!"

I never really bought into her constant comment "Be Somebody," but that constant admonition of the "shoulds" buried itself in me and led to a lot of false guilt and sense of shame.

I realized this deep lie in my spirit when I became a real Christian, but the aftermath still hung around for an opportunity to demean and discourage me.

At this point in my life, I was letting my old "shoulds" hamper the ministry I could have with the Women of the Church, trying to not offend them (my perception) and impose on them expectations from my spiritual experiences. I had an undefined longing to be free of all my "shoulds" and just be the self that God had created with the gifts He had put and now risen in me.

Like high tide battering against the wall of my will, I was inwardly defeated and discouraged. Maybe the best term for how I was feeling is "burnout!"

What does all of this have to do with coming to the Spurs?

It has to do with Jesus reaching down and pulling me out of the pit and setting my feet in a wide place! My "wide place" was to be with/in this group of women, the Spurs. That "wide place" represented freedom, safety and room to grow and for me, a place where restoration would begin.

Spurred by Grace
Chapter Eight

A Time to Travel

A Time to Spread Our Wings
Spurs on the Go!
by Molly Dummit

Where you go I will go, and where you stay I will stay.
Your people will be my people and your God my God.
Ruth 1:16

*O*ur monthly meetings were just not enough.
 We loved to take day trips, have slumber parties, overnights, and retreats. We also took longer trips together, both domestically and internationally.

Here are some of these fun times to assist our own memories and to give others ideas of different things to do and places to go together.

DAY TRIPS:
 Agape Force Ranch (Lindale, Texas)
 Azalea Trail (Tyler, Texas)
 Lunch with Mrs. Talkington (Tyler, Texas)
 Lunch with Trudy (Tyler, Texas)
 Adolphus Hotel for lunch (Dallas, Texas)
 Mansion Hotel for lunch (Dallas, Texas)
 Swiss Ave home for lunch (Dallas, Texas)
 Chocolate Angel Restaurant for lunch (Dallas, Texas)

SLUMBER PARTIES FOR SPURS:
Molly Dummit's home (twice)
Sally Renshaw's home (twice)
Georgia Smith's home (twice)
Gayle O'Neal's home (twice)
Carolyn Boyd's home (three times)
Ann Hyde's home (once)
Clarice Townes Miller's home. (Spring 1997)

OVERNIGHT TRIPS OUT OF TOWN:
Nutt House (Granbury, Texas)
Pecan Plantation (Granbury, Texas)
Godfrey's Place (Lake Granbury, Texas) Molly's sixtieth birthday! 1988
Bridgeport, Texas (one bath and 10 women!)
Adolphus Hotel (Dallas, Texas)
Embassy Suites (DFW Airport) Mother-Daughter retreat February 2002

RETREATS:
Carolyn Boyd's lake house (Granbury, Texas) Very first get-together in 1977!
Pat Reynold's house (Pineville, Missouri) Three times!
Kathleen Page Clark's home (Horseshoe Bay, Texas) Once for the single Spurs (November 2003) and once for all Spurs (April 2008)
Living Waters (Kerrville, Texas)
Clarice Townes Miller's home (Nacogdoches, Texas) (November 1999 and April 2003)
Mary Guenzel's home (near Colorado Springs, Colorado) September, 2003 and 2004
Elizabeth Buckley's home (Lexington, Kentucky) April 1997
Friend's home (Salado, Texas)

DOMESTIC TRAVEL:

Carolyn Boyd's condo (Eagle-Vail, Colorado)

Jointly (Carolyn Boyd and Gayle O'Neal) owned condo (Beaver Creek, Colorado) Three times!

Kathleen Page Clark's home (Los Gatos, California)

Phyllis White's condo (Park City, Utah)

Virginia Kahler's home (Santa Fe, New Mexico) August 2000

Camp DeSoto (Mentone, Alabama) April 2001

Lillian Farms Bed and Breakfast (Washington, Texas) April 2005

Keith and DeAnn Boyd's home (New York, New York)

INTERNATIONAL TRAVEL:

Eight Spurs go to the Cotswolds with many side trips (England) June 1990

Sixteen Spurs go to the Medici summer villa and vineyards (Tuscany area, Italy) April 1998

Slumber party at Clarice Townes Miller's in
Nacogdoches, Texas. Spring 1997.
Left to right: Sandra Talkington, Gayle O'Neal, Carolyn Boyd,
Molly Dummit, Carolyn Driggers Mallone, Clarice Townes Miller,
Mimi Mack.

The Spurs leaving the Mildred B. Cooper
Memorial Chapel in Bella Vista, Arkansas. October 1998.

The Spurs in Horseshoe Bay Resort hot tub, Horseshoe Bay, Texas.
April 2008.
Left to right back row: Molly Dummit, Sandra Talkington,
Kathleen Page Clark, Clarice Townes Miller, Sally Renshaw.
Left to right front row: Phyllis White,
Mary Alice Brumley, Mimi Mack.

Left to right: Sally Renshaw, Mimi Mack, Molly Dummit,
Horseshoe Bay, Texas. April 2008.

The Spurs (eating again!) in Lexington, Kentucky. April 1997.

The Spurs in Deer Valley listening to the Utah Symphony.
January 2002.

The Spurs were picked up at the San Jose airport in a limousine to
come to Kathleen's in Los Gatos, California. September 1994.

Nacogdoches retreat at the Miller home. November 1999
Left to right: Georgia Smith, Virginia Kahler, Maureen Eagan,
Kathleen Page Clark, Elizabeth Buckley

A handful of Spurs in New York City. June 2009.
Left to right: Harriet Wallace, Mary Alice Brumley, Molly Dummit,
Sandra Talkington, Carolyn Boyd, Sally Renshaw, Mimi Mack

Left to right: Carolyn Boyd, Barbara Clarkin, Kathleen Page Clark, Carolyn Driggers Mallone. Cotswolds, England. June 1990.

Left to right: Sally Renshaw, Molly Dummit, Sandra Talkington and Pat Reynolds. Cotswolds, England. June 1990.

The Spurs gathered in a field of mustard in the Tuscany area of Italy.
April 1998

The Spurs stayed a week at the Medici summer home in
Tuscany, Italy. April 1998

A Time to Retreat

by Barbara Clarkin

Only fear the LORD, and serve him faithfully with all your heart.
For consider what great things he has done for you.
1 Samuel 12:24 (ESV)

The Spurs love to travel together and always look forward to the quality time that retreats provide. When thinking about when and where we might go, I mentioned that I had a friend, Mary, who had a beautiful retreat home that slept a lot of people and was located in the Rocky Mountains of Colorado. I called Mary and asked her if she would be open to hosting the Spurs. She welcomed the idea with graciousness and enthusiasm. She would not consider payment from us. As far as she was concerned, the Lord meant for her to use the property to further His work. She welcomed the idea of a Christian group of women having a gathering with her.

When we learned that her home slept twenty-two people, we had the idea of including our daughters. We wanted them to spend more time with the Spurs and experience what a wonderfully supportive group of Christian women could mean in their lives. Perhaps they would be encouraged to start a group.

Not as many Spurs and their daughters could attend as we had hoped. Scheduling retreats is always a challenge but we knew that it would be meaningful for those who could be there. Six Spurs, five daughters and Mary, our host, were in for an intimate and special time together. The retreat was so wonderful that the following year we went to Mary's again with eleven Spurs and two daughters.

After six months of planning, the time finally arrived for the Spurs first trip to Mary's home. The eleven of us flew into Colorado Springs at two different times. I was part of the first group that gathered early in the morning at the Dallas/Ft Worth airport on the Thursday after Labor Day, 2003. We were blessed to arrive early enough to have lunch at the Broadmoor Hotel in Colorado Springs. What delicious food, a beautiful setting and a fun way to begin our time together.

Since I was in the first group to arrive in Colorado Springs, we had the envelope of money that was collected ahead of time to spend on groceries. I was amused at the amount of food the others thought was needed for only a four-day retreat since I was the one who had raised and fed seven children and their friends. We were able to bless Mary with a lot of extra food when we left!

After purchasing our groceries, we continued our drive through Pike National Forest to our destination at ten thousand feet. As we approached Mary's house, we were amazed at her majestic mountain home and her surrounding pastoral setting. There was a bridge over a pond near the entrance to the main house. Mary was on the porch with a huge grin to greet us. She had not met any of the other Spurs and yet we felt she had known each of us a long time. What a gracious and selfless hostess!

We entered the house and immediately sounded like a choir singing "Ohs and Ahs." Large windows framed the beauty of the surrounding mountains, forests, sky and clouds in all directions. Porches and balconies provided an uninterrupted view of Pikes Peak. We were surrounded on three sides with panoramic views of the Pike National Forest.

Mary purchased this beautiful home and majestic property in 1999. It was originally designed as a retreat for a church. All the rooms were large. We were intrigued that each room had different ceiling decors. The bedrooms and baths were scattered throughout the multi-level home. There were signs over each bedroom doorway with a name of a Saint and the name of one of her children or grandchildren. I felt the presence of the Holy

Spirit in her home, which did not surprise me since Mary was a devoted Christian and devout Catholic!

The home included a small intimate chapel, an extensive media room with a wide selection of classic movies to watch, a physical fitness room and a hot tub. I asked her how she managed to furnish all 22,000 square feet of the house since she had moved from a much smaller home. She replied, "The Salvation Army, Goodwill Industries and St. Vincent de Paul's Association!"

Mary had created in the woods surrounding the home, many areas of interest. Situated among the tall trees was a path with the fourteen Stations of the Cross. There was also a full-size teepee for her grandchildren. A mini-amphitheater was constructed for outdoor services. A separate building housed a full kitchen. We were very amused that what appeared to be an outhouse, was actually a modern bathroom furnished with a hanging chandelier and red velvet wallpaper!

Another building on the property slept twelve. Mary was a planner and a dreamer. Mary talked of future plans to remodel the building to include meeting rooms. She also has plans to construct a separate chapel building to accommodate a larger group of people.

When the second group of Spurs arrived later that afternoon, there was another round of "Ohs and Ahs." We had the first night's meal planned, but little did the Spurs know what a treat they had in store for them. Our daughters decided that they would prepare the meals as a gift to their mothers during the retreat. It takes a good bit of work to prepare meals for a large group. What a precious gift of service! The daughters were caught up in the spirit of the Spurs.

The mothers and daughters spent the next three days immersed in faith sharing, praying, eating and celebrating a birthday. There was a perfect balance of togetherness and alone time. We enjoyed our time inside the home, often gathered around the beautiful rock fireplace, as well as time outside where we enjoyed walks in the beautiful surroundings of nature.

On Sunday, we lingered with our coffee out on the deck one last time before leaving our mountain top experience. The early morning sun was outlining Pikes Pike in spectacular beauty and color. We all agreed we were in God's country and in God's presence. We had a special closing devotional where we went around the room and gave each other a blessing. The Spurs left feeling pampered, loved and spiritually enriched. The daughters were all blessed and inspired after spending time with us. We unanimously agreed that Mary was now an honorary Spur. We drove away with a memorable, breathtaking view of Pikes Peak against a glorious blue sky. Thank you, Mary, and thank you, God, for this refreshing retreat. We give Him all the glory!

A 2013 update:

Mary's place has now been turned into a seventy-acre retreat center. It is called *El Tesoro de Los Angeles*. Below is more information about Mary and the retreat center as well as the retreat website so that you can see how Mary's dream continues. God bless Mary!

Mary W. Guenzel

A native of Denver, Colorado, Mary W. Guenzel spent most of her life in Ft. Worth, Texas. Feeling the call to return to Colorado, Mary returned in the early '90s where she purchased and rehabilitated the house, which today is known as "Annunciation Hall."

After Mary completed the rehabilitation of her home, she began to use the property for a larger good. She would go on to purchase the two surrounding properties giving her approximately seventy forested acres for the purpose of opening up a retreat center.

Since she began this effort, dozens of churches and organizations and hundreds of people have experienced El Tesoro de los Angeles Retreat Center. Mary continues to use her personal resources to grow the Retreat Center and to improve the guests' experience. Upon completion of the final two projects (San Francisco Javier Chapel and St. Mary Hall and Conference Center), Mary will leave a lasting legacy by donating all the property and its buildings to the Nuestra Senora de la Paz Foundation, which will carry out the mission of El Tesoro de los Angeles for the years ahead.

http://eltesororetreat.org

A Time to be Chosen
Chosen for One Another
by Phyllis White

*You did not choose me, but I chose you
and appointed you to go and bear fruit — fruit that will last.
John 15:16   (NIV 1984)*

When Mimi invited me to go on a trip with the Spurs to Italy, no one on this earth could have guessed what was in store for me. The invitation came at a time when I was lower than a snake. After having been in the retail business for thirty-six years, we had just gone out of business and in a way I had lost my identity. Not only that, but my dad was in a facility in the final stages of Alzheimer's dementia while my mother was in another facility having had her second mastectomy and then a stroke paralyzing her on the left side. My dad didn't know anything, including any members of his family, and my mother was bedridden and most unhappy. I say all this not for your sympathy, but rather to explain how low I was at this particular time in my life. Also, I might add, I am an only child, so all the care of and decisions for my parents fell on my shoulders, which was no small job, emotionally or physically.

I had been on my knees begging God for help and He sent me on a trip to Tuscany with a group of loving Christian women to comfort me. When I mentioned the trip to Bob, my husband, he insisted I go and assured me he would take care of everything on the home front, which he did. There were sixteen of us on the trip and we did not all go on the same plane or even on the same day, but the plan was for all of us to meet up in Venice.

In the Spur group, there was a beautiful, loving redheaded woman named Carolyn Driggers Mallone, who was in the beginning stages of Alzheimer's dementia. She was a very best friend with Sandra Talkington, who had taken it on herself to care for and be responsible for Carolyn. The only problem was that they were not on the same flight going to Europe so Molly was to be her surrogate caregiver until Sandra connected up with us.

All was going well until we were boarding the train headed for Venice. Somehow Carolyn and I got separated from the entire group. (Looking back, I feel sure it was due to schlepping too much luggage, not speaking Italian or maybe being too slow!).

We had a couple of hours on the train and then we arrived in Venice, the end of the line. Well, I was in a foreign country, couldn't speak the language, had no idea where we were staying and in charge of a person who might wander off if I took my eyes off her.

After some arrow prayers, I finally tied her to a post with my Chanel scarf, so at least she was tied in style, piled the luggage around her and went to try to find an English-speaking person who could help us. Just as I was leaving, here came the rest of the group and I was never so glad to see anyone!

We had a fun time in Venice dining, shopping, sightseeing and then left for our villa in Tuscany. The Villa was built in the eighteenth century and had been used as a hunting lodge by the Medici family. It had a charming chapel (a separate building), a vineyard, olive trees, an olive press, a houseboy and most importantly, a cook. We stayed there six glorious days.

Every morning our driver, Giovanni, who spoke no English, would arrive along with our English-speaking guide and we would tour a nearby town. On the way, we sang, "Father protect us, Father protect us, Father in Heaven protect us." As you know, Italians are not the sanest drivers and some of the roads are narrow and precarious, but protect us He did and every evening when we arrived safely back to the villa, we sang "Father we thank you, Father we thank you, Father in Heaven we thank you."

Happily, I had become a part of the Spurs and have been blessed with their prayers and friendship. Even though I am the new girl on the block, they never fail to show up in traumatic times, like when my parents died. Here came the Spurs....even those who now lived out of town.

I feel privileged to be a part of this faithful, loving group. In the *Four Loves*, C.S. Lewis writes:

But as for a Christian, there are, strictly speaking, no chances. A secret Master of the Ceremonies has been at work. Christ, who said to the disciples 'Ye have not chosen me, but I have chosen you,' can truly say to every group of Christian friends, 'You have not chosen one another, but I have chosen you for one another.' The friendship is not a reward for our discrimination and good taste in finding one another out. It is the instrument by which God reveals to each the beauties of all the others.

I thank God that He chose me to be a Spur.

Left to right: Molly Dummit, Mimi Mack, Phyllis White
and Carolyn Driggers Mallone.

Spurred by Grace
Chapter Nine

A Time to Serve

A Time to Make a Difference

Collective volunteer services done by the Spurs
through the years
(Listed alphabetically and anonymously by ministry)

Serve the LORD with gladness!
Come into his presence with singing!
Psalm 100:2 (ESV)

The spur is a reminder of Hebrew 10:24.

Bible Study Fellowship (BSF)
Teaching Leader
Assistant Teaching Leader
Group Leaders
Children's Leader
Treasurer

Board Members of:
All Church Home for Children (Fort Worth, Texas)
All Saints Hospital Foundation Board (Fort Worth, Texas)
Arlington Civic Chorus (Arlington, Texas)
Christian Women's Job Corps (Fort Worth, Texas)
Cornerstone Assistance Network: for the homeless and needy
    (Fort Worth, Texas)
Denton Christian Preschool, President (Denton, Texas)
Fort Worth Symphony (Fort Worth, Texas)
Harris Hospital Kupferle Cancer Board (Fort Worth, Texas)
Junior League (Fort Worth, Texas)
Kappa Alpha Theta Alumnae Board (Fort Worth, Texas)
Love in the Name of Christ, President (Nacogdoches, Texas)
Samaritan Counseling Center, President (Nacogdoches, Texas)
Texas Christian University Fine Arts Guild (Fort Worth, Texas)
Van Cliburn Foundation (Fort Worth, Texas)
Women's Auxiliary of the Salvation Army (Fort Worth, Texas)
YMCA Board (Arlington, Texas)
YWCA Board (Fort Worth, Texas)
YWCA Foundation Board (Fort Worth, Texas)

Chaplain:
Marketplace Ministries (Fort Worth, Texas)
Plaza Medical Center and Harris Southwest Hospital (Fort
    Worth, Texas)

Church leadership:
Elder of Presbyterian Church, U.S.A. (Denton, Texas)
Moderator of Presbyterian Women, U.S.A. (Denton and
    Nacogdoches, Texas)

Chair of the Building and Grounds; ten-year visionary plan for St. Andrew Catholic Church (Fort Worth, Texas)

Chair of the Pastoral Council for St. Andrew Catholic Church (Fort Worth, Texas)

Church prayer team (Marble Falls, Texas)

Editors of Church paper (Dallas and Grapevine, Texas)

Lay healing prayer ministry team (Dallas, Texas)

Missions planning group (Lexington, Kentucky)

Personal Faith and Family Life chairperson (Dallas, Texas)

St. Andrew Catholic Church Funeral Ministry team (Fort Worth, Texas)

Stephen Ministry leader (Arlington, Texas)

Tuesday night worship leader (Lexington, Kentucky)

Hosting:

Pastor and wife when their church of two hundred relocated after hurricane Katrina (Horseshoe Bay, Texas)

Van Cliburn International Competitions competitors (Fort Worth, Texas)

Mentoring:

Children in Como Elementary School, weekly (Fort Worth, Texas)

Elementary school children (Fort Worth, Texas)

International students (Fort Worth and Horseshoe Bay, Texas)

Re-Engage; coaching couples in church setting (Dallas, Texas)

Retreat speaker (Fort Worth, Texas)

Spiritual Director (Rockwall, Texas)

World Missionary Baptist Church tutoring (Fort Worth, Texas)

Young Moms (Marble Falls, Texas)

Mission Trips:

Church Mission trip to Quito, Ecuador (Fort Worth, Texas)

Dental mission trips to Costa Rica, Ecuador, Honduras, Peru and Romania (Horseshoe Bay and Rockwall, Texas)

Gardening and Charities to Santa Fe, New Mexico (Arlington, Texas)

Medical trips to Africa, Bulgaria, Copper Canyon, Mexico, Guatemala, Russia (Fort Worth, Texas and Lexington, Kentucky)

Mission trip to Romania

Training trips to China, Honduras, Russia (Dallas, Texas)

One of the Organizers:

Auxiliary for Union Gospel Mission (Fort Worth, Texas)

Jane Marshall School; for children with learning differences (Denton, Texas)

The Followers; a prayer and support group for over thirty years (Dallas, Texas)

Presidents of:

Auxiliary to the Tarrant County Medical Society (Fort Worth, Texas)

Christian Prayer Breakfast (Fort Worth, Texas)

Home and School Association, St. Andrew Catholic Church (Fort Worth, Texas)

Jewel Charity (Fort Worth, Texas)

Mid-Cities Pan-Hellenic (Arlington, Texas)

Salvation Army Service Unit chairman (Decatur, Texas)

Texas Girls' Choir (Fort Worth, Texas)

Women of Rotary (Fort Worth, Texas)

Women of the Church; Presbyterian women's organization (Dallas, Texas)

Prison Ministries:

Book Ministry, Dawson County Jail; taking the Chaplain's Christian books into the women's jail pods (Dallas, Texas)

Queens:

Two Cotton Bowl queens! (from Fort Worth and Decatur, Texas)

Teachers:
Alpha Course (Fort Worth, Texas)
English tutor (Arlington, Texas)
Morningside Elementary School music (Fort Worth, Texas)
Non-English speaking children (Fort Worth, Texas)
Speech pathologist (Fort Worth, Texas)
Sunday School (every city a Spur lives!)
Vacation Bible School (many Spurs!)

Volunteers for:
Allen Chapel (Fort Worth, Texas)
Bread Basket Ministries
Cooks Children Medical Center (Fort Worth, Texas)
Covenant Hospice (Fort Worth, Texas)
Habitat for Humanity; building homes for needy(Fort Worth and Nacogdoches, Texas)
Laura's Lunch Committee; raise money for Baylor All Saints Hospital Neurology Dept. (Fort Worth, Texas)
Love in the Name of Christ (Nacogdoches, Texas)
Masonic Home Monthly birthday parties (Arlington, Texas)
Meals on Wheels (Arlington and Fort Worth, Texas)
Mission Arlington Alpha Day Care; rocking babies (Arlington, Texas)
Opera Guild (Fort Worth, Texas)
Presbyterian Synod Hunger Action Enabler (Denton, Texas)
Salvation Army Service Center (Fort Worth, Texas)
Stephen Ministry caregiver (Arlington and Dallas, Texas)
St. Andrew Catholic Church Nursing Home and Assisted Living Ministry (Fort Worth, Texas)
St. Andrew Catholic Church Pastoral Care Committee (Fort Worth, Texas)
Tarrant Net (Fort Worth, Texas)
Union Gospel Mission (Fort Worth, Texas)
Wise Choices Pregnancy Resource Center (Decatur, Texas)
YMCA (Fort Worth, Texas)
YWCA (Fort Worth, Texas)

Youth Ministries:
- Bluebird Leader (Fort Worth, Texas)
- Boy Scout Leader (Fort Worth, Texas)
- Campaign for high school girls (Fort Worth, Texas)
- Campfire Girls (Fort Worth, Texas)
- Child Evangelism (Fort Worth, Texas)
- Den mother for Cub Scouts (Fort Worth, Texas)
- Denton Christian Preschool (Denton, Texas)
- Good New Club (Fort Worth, Texas)
- Morningside Elementary School music (Ft. Worth, Texas)
- North High Mount and Como Elementary School coordinator for art work (Fort Worth, Texas)
- Nursery worker
- Sunday School teachers
- Teen Challenge (Arlington and Fort Worth, Texas)
- Vacation Bible School leaders and workers
- Young Life
- Youth advisor (Dallas, Texas)

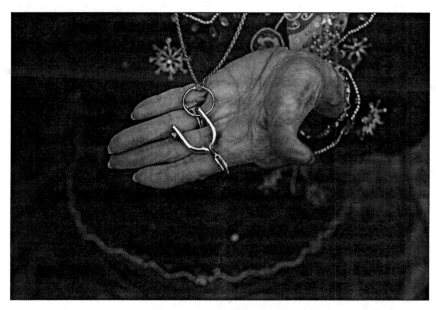

Georgia Smith's husband gifted and blessed each of us
with a silver spur.

A Time to be Sent
Send Me
by Kathleen Page Clark

Then I heard the voice of the Lord saying,
"Whom shall I send? And who will go for us?"
And I said, "Here am I. Send me!"
Isaiah 6:8

It had been my prayer and my heart's desire for many years to go on mission trips.

I retired as a passenger service agent with a major airline. I knew that I could get to wherever I needed to go to do mission work for free or for very little money. It was the cost of the land portion of mission trips that was still beyond my budget as a retired single woman.

A retired periodontist, Dr. William Sasser, started an organization under the umbrella of the Christian Medical and Dental Association called Dental Community Fellowship. He and his wife Susalee, both dear friends of mine, have been taking dentists, dental students and support workers all over the world almost every month since his retirement.

One day, out of the blue, he called me on the phone and said "I have just planned a trip to Lima, Peru, in June of 2008 and this is the trip for you to go on, Kathleen. It is time to get off your knees and to get on the airplane." The ground cost for the week was going to be $600. I had heard rumors that President Bush was going to send everyone a $600 economic stimulus check. Yes, sign me up! I may not be stimulating the United States economy by going on my first mission trip to Lima, Peru, but surely I would be stimulating God's economy!

Before the mission trip, I invited the Spurs to my home in central Texas for a long weekend retreat. Our daylong gatherings are wonderful but it is even more special when we can spend extended periods of time together. During our "prayer and praise" time, I was telling them of answered prayer and that I was signed up to go on my first mission trip. They shared in my excitement and before departing, they gathered around me and prayed over me as a "send off."

After the Spurs left, my heart and home were still resonating with their presence and the Lord's Spirit. I just sat and stared out at the lake with gratitude for the lives of each one of these ladies, many of whom I had known for over twenty years. The heart connection that we have for each other as a result of our God connection is amazing. After a time of silent praise, I got up and aimlessly walked around the house to check to be sure nothing was left behind.

Leave it to the Spurs! Without even telling me (and probably each other), there were six one hundred dollar bills secretly tucked away in a number of special places: on my pillow, beside my bed and in an envelope on my desk. Sweet one-liner love notes said things like "I just want to be a part of your first mission trip" and "God bless you on your first mission trip." Needless to say, I was touched to the point of tears!

Why am I not surprised that the love offerings came to exactly $600! God is so good! I used that money to go on my first mission trip, at the young age of sixty-six. Oh, what an incredible time I had. I had always regretted that I did not have a skill to be used on the mission field, as doctors, nurses and translators have, but I quickly learned that for every dentist, it takes at least two support people to help them so that they can do their work. The dental instruments need sterilizing, there is medicine to package up and dispense, there are children to play with while their parents have dental work done, there are people who need their head and hands held during procedures, there are those comforted by prayer, there are opportunities to tell others about Jesus and the whole world needs more hugs (my specialty!).

Eventually, the $600 economic stimulus check did arrive and I was able to use it to go on my second mission trip to Honduras in December of 2008.

In faith, I also signed up to go to Ecuador in March of 2009 with the Dental Community Fellowship. By this time, I had learned to trust God in His provisions, a wonderful and needed reminder for not just mission trips, but all of life!

Mission work is my calling. Sharing God's extravagant love with smiles and hugs are my gifts! I am living proof that God does not call you to do something without equipping and supplying what is needed to pursue the call.

Thank you, Spurs, for not only providing the financial means to send me out on my first mission trip, but for continually blessing me, sustaining me with prayer, undergirding me with encouragement and emotional support. As writer Joyce Landorf would say, "You are my balcony people." You are always there to cheer me on.

Thank you for sharing in the excitement of my newfound passion. You are wind to my Spirit.

A Time to be Lifted Up
Salvation Army Speech and Implications for Today
by Gayle O'Neal

When Moses' hands grew tired, they took a stone
and put it under him and he sat on it.
Aaron and Hur held his hands up
—one on one side, one on the other—
so that his hands remained steady till sunset.
Exodus 17:12

Many years ago I was asked to speak at the Salvation Army Ladies luncheon. I have long forgotten the speech but have never forgotten the heart of the message.

The message came from Exodus 17:8-15. The Israelites were being attacked by the Amalekites, a fierce and dreadful army. Moses sent some men out to fight them with the promise, "I will stand on top of the hill with the staff of God in my hands."

As long as Moses held up his hands, the Israelites were winning but whenever he lowered his hands, the Amalekites were winning.

Just as we do in life's battles, Moses grew tired and his hands grew weary, but "Aaron and Hur came alongside him, put a rock under him and held his hands up, one on one side, one on the other, so his hands remained steady until sunset."

So Joshua overcame the Amalekite army with the sword.

Then Moses built an altar and called it "The Lord is my Banner." He said, "For hands were lifted up to the throne of the Lord."

Although this was part of a speech to the Salvation Army Auxiliary, it embodies the "heart" of the Spurs.

When we fight the battles of life, we become exhausted and then we realize we are surrounded by one another coming "alongside" and lifting us up and we become victorious.

The Lord is our Banner—Jehovah Nissi.

A Time of Interruption
An Unexpected Interruption
by Clarice Townes Miller

Do not neglect to show hospitality to strangers,
for by doing that some have entertained angels
without knowing it.
Hebrews 13:2

The phone rang. I had only about ten minutes before I had to dash out the door to start the afternoon carpool. I almost didn't answer it, but an inner voice urged me to answer.

It was my good friend who was a counselor and there was urgency in her voice. "Do you have a few minutes to talk?" she asked. "I have a problem and wondered if you could help me with it. I have a client that has nowhere to go."

"What do you mean?" I asked.

"She was sent to me and since I've been talking to her I've found out how desperate her situation is. She and her eighteen-month-old son have been living in her car for the past several days. Since the temperature is forecasted to be freezing tonight I don't feel I can let her go." I listened as she told me how this young mother had had to leave an abusive situation so that neither she nor her son would continue to be in danger. She had been referred to my friend and now she was calling me to help her think of where she could send her.

All I knew was that I had three children that would be waiting for me at school and I wondered what I could possibly do to help in this situation. Suddenly I realized I was blurting out, "Well, we have an extra bedroom downstairs and they could stay with us overnight."

"That would help," she said, "but she needs to work and they need a place to stay for several months while she saves enough money so that she can get back on her feet."

"O.K., we'll work something out," I answered.

"Thanks so much—one more thing—she needs someone to keep John while she works at night and sleeps during the day."

"We will see how this works out and don't you be far away!" I teased.

As I drove to pick up our children, I thought, *"What have I just agreed to do? I haven't even talked to my husband about it? Our days are so full how could we possibly do one more thing?"* Had I completely lost my mind? Then I took several deep breaths and thought, *"I can't believe this little boy's name is John. How interesting!"* Our oldest son, John, had gone to college just weeks before. I wasn't prepared for the hole in my heart that was there since our son had left. There was an absence of one who had meant so much to us and now he was spreading his wings. I knew that was a natural and necessary part of his growing up but I hadn't realized how a mother's heart would feel. *"Was this God's way of trying to ease my pain? Did I have any idea what I had just agreed to do?"*

After I went to bed that night it dawned on me that I had agreed to let a stranger come into our home and stay in the downstairs bedroom while our family was upstairs. She could have taken anything that she had wanted from us. I knew nothing about her except that she was a person in need. I prayed that God would calm my spirit and help me not be afraid of what might happen. I had to pray that prayer several times as the days turned into weeks and then months.

That next Monday morning we had a Spurs meeting in Arlington, Texas. I could hardly wait to get there to share this unbelievable story. I asked them for their prayers so that this would be a blessing for all of us. My friends listened as I told this story of wonder.

We grew to love John and his mother. She was hardly ever around us because she was either working or sleeping. I told her that we would care for John so that she could work. Wherever we went we took John with us and he quickly became a part of our family. Surprisingly, my husband was delighted to have this "bundle of energy" interrupt our lives so unexpectedly. He helped care for the baby when I was busy with our other children.

It was at the first husband and wife get-together of the Spurs that I realized what an impact this child was having on my husband. We shared that night things we appreciated about our husbands. It was a delightful, quite hysterically funny and insightful night as we showed our appreciation for our husbands. I shared how much it had meant to me that he had been so willing and agreeable to taking in strangers. He had helped me with the baby and been so willing to help this young lady who had been so afraid when she first came to us. As I talked, he interrupted to tell more of the story and as he finished, he had tears flowing down his cheeks. Perhaps because my husband was adopted, this experience tapped a deep core within him.

The young mother and her son stayed with us for four months until she had saved enough money to get a small apartment. We never felt that we got to know her well because she was busy but we grew to love John. One day she came and told us that she was leaving and thanked us for what we had offered. As quickly as she came into our lives, she was gone.

Some years later when John was ten, my friend, the counselor, got a Christmas card from his mother saying that she was married, living in Arkansas and that John was doing very well in school. She asked my friend to call and tell us this good news. That was the last time we heard from her.

As I reflect back on that period in our lives, how blessed we were to have this unexpected interruption! We had been asked to help someone in need. By doing that we received many blessings.

Is this not the meaning of the Christmas story? "O God, continue to interrupt our lives with your blessings and open our eyes to see, ears to hear and voices to speak for You. In the name of the One who interrupted many lives years ago and continues to do so today. Amen."

Clarice's husband, Hamp Miller, walking with baby John.

A Time to Grow Old Together
by Kathleen Page Clark

I was young and now I am old, yet I have never seen
the righteous forsaken or their children begging bread.
Psalm 37:25

It is said that a picture is worth a thousand words!
You can only imagine how many hundreds of pictures we
went through to illustrate some of the stories in this book and
to capture the spirit of the thirty-five years that the Spurs have
been together.

There are just a few special group photos that we wanted to
include as living proof that we have indeed grown old together.

These pictures are especially meaningful to us as some of the
members are already in Heaven. The rest of us are Heaven bound!

An early Spur photo taken in Colorado in 1984.

Left to right standing: Pat Reynolds, Kathleen Page Clark,
a Spur friend, Mary Jo Scheideman, Maureen Eagan,
Carolyn Driggers Mallone, Sandra Talkington,
Clarice Townes Miller.
Left to right back row: Mimi Mack, Molly Dummit.

The last Spur Christmas at the Scheideman home in 2011.

Left to right seated: Mary Jo Scheideman, Carol Williams, Anne Hyde.
Left to right front row on stairs: Gayle O'Neal, Sandra Talkington,
Pat Reynolds, Maureen Eagan, Sally Renshaw,
Mimi Mack, Molly Dummit.*eft to right back row on stairs:* Carolyn Boyd, Harriet Wallace,
Mary Alice Brumley, Clarice Townes Miller, Phyllis White,
Kathleen Page Clark, Barbara Clarkin.

A Time to Finish Strong

by Kathleen Page Clark

They will still bear fruit in old age,
they will stay fresh and green.
Psalm 92:14

The gift of living out our Christian life with the Spurs has been a real gift for each of us. We are thankful that God has mysteriously brought our lives together and that we have had such dear friends with which to share this earthly life. It is becoming more and more apparent, that we all have more years to look back on, than to look ahead to, on this earth. Eternity is nearing. This scripture in Proverbs is a hopeful reminder.

And she smiles at the future.
Proverbs 31:25 (NASB)

With our years of being together, it often takes the entire group to piece together our history. We have been together so long, that we just have to say a word or phrase to evoke a hearty laugh, a funny story or a painful memory. We live in the world of "remember when."

Some of our memories are better than others. It is sometimes a hard reality, and sometimes even hurtful to others, that we can't recall things as before. That is a reality check on the aging process that takes patience with ourselves and others.

However, our gatherings now are not just about remembering. We want to finish strong. Even in our later years, we look to each

204

other to help with new issues: health problems, downsizing our households, new family situations. We deal with losses of all kinds, whether it is a best friend, a family member, our glasses or our hair.

We all want our lives to be a legacy to God's faithfulness to the very end.

With God's help, the support of the Spurs, and each of our own local churches, we want to continue to be glory reflectors of our mighty Lord and Savior. We want to continue to age with grace and humor. With God's help, and the assurance of His promises, we are confident we will do so.

In our later years, we particularly count on this promise:

Even to your old age and gray hairs I am He, I am He who will sustain you.
I have made you and I will carry you;
I will sustain you and I will rescue you.
   Isaiah 46:4

God keeps His promises!

Three Spur hands.

Spurred by Grace
Chapter Ten

A Time for Redemption

A Time to be Adopted	by Mimi Mack
A Time to Choose	by Gayle O'Neal
A Time to Redeem	by Pat Reynolds
A Time for Mercy	by Pat Reynolds
A Time to Reflect	by Pat (and Bob) Reynolds
A Time to Rest	by Pat Reynolds

A Time to be Adopted

by Mimi Mack

Long before he laid down earth's foundations,
he had us in mind, had settled on us as the focus of his love,
to be made whole and holy by his love.
Long, long ago he decided to adopt us into his family
through Jesus Christ.
Ephesians 1:5-6 (The Message)

I had a wonderful childhood with love, a great education, friends, and lacked nothing the world could offer. I attended church faithfully and always wanted to know God. Deep inside, I knew there was something missing. It was Christmas 1966 and I heard the Plan of Salvation for the very first time. It struck my heart like an arrow. I knew finally what was missing in me. I accepted the free gift that Jesus offered and became new from the inside out immediately.

My life from that point has truly been a Cinderella story. Like Cinderella, I was in a lost and hopeless situation that I could not change. I was spiritually poverty ridden. Then, wonder of wonders, God Almighty reached His hand down from Heaven, picked me out of the ashes and called me "His own child."

Imagine how I felt to be adopted by a King. I was the one He wanted for His daughter. He chose me personally. I wasn't rescued because I deserved it, but because God is gracious and gives freely. I only had to accept what He gave me. Only He could have seen a princess through my dirty rags. He calls me lovely things like "Holy" and "Blameless." My life on that day changed completely, forever! He put His Royal Seal on me—and in me—so everyone in heaven and earth would know that I was a part of His family. He wrote me a wonderful love letter, the Bible, telling me all about Himself. He told me about the wonderful place in His palace in Heaven that He was preparing for me. He introduced me to His only Son—and said we would surely become best friends. Because I was miraculously rescued and adopted, I wanted my Father and Brother to be pleased with me. I must live by their family standards. I must shed my old ways like a snake sheds its old skin. I have a beautiful new Robe of Righteousness so I can leave the rags behind.

I have
- a new name
- a new family
- a new chance
- a clean slate.

I have been
- saved by grace
- saved by mercy
- saved by love.

I love to tell others my Good News about the unspeakable riches that my Father has lavished on me. I am now God's earthly dwelling place
- His Holy of Holies
- His Temple.

Imagine that!!!!

For these reasons, I kneel before my Father to ask Him for His power to be the person that will honor His household. Part of that process was becoming a Spur.

A Time to Choose

by Gayle O'Neal

You will keep in perfect peace him whose mind is steadfast,
because he trusts in you.
Isaiah 26:3 (NIV 1984)

telephone call came about three o'clock in the afternoon and, as I listened, I sank to my knees on the hard kitchen floor. I had just received some heartbreaking news about one of my children—my prodigal child.

Have you ever watched and prayed in anguish over a beloved child, as they chose the way of darkness rather than the path of life, as they removed themselves from under your umbrella of protection?

Have you ever had your heart turn to ice in fear when you realized they were not only throwing away all you had dreamed for them, but they were putting themselves in danger?

I was prostrate on the floor crying out to God. He had given this child into our care and we had failed.

Over and over again, I pleaded for God to forgive the failure of my husband and me. I could not stop begging. I was reminded over and over again of the mistakes, the anger, the frustration and the hurtful things we had said to her in the past. I cried. I beat the floor and I cried some more.

Then, in a small still voice in my spirit, I heard these words, "Get up and refrain from crying, you have done far more right than you have done wrong and you have already confessed these things and you have already been forgiven. Remember, I am not the accuser."

I knew this in my heart, because of the Scriptures, that God readily forgives confessed sin and that He is not the accuser of the brethren. I knew that He was my adviser, my guide, but not my accuser. The accuser of the brethren is Satan and he was having a "heyday" with me.

Then the battle began and I was in spiritual warfare. I had to take this new awareness and let it overtake the fear in my mind. The battle was fierce, but God set me free.

God had one more lesson for me that day, and in my spirit, I clearly saw a tightrope: on one side was faith and on the other side was fear. On the side of faith was life and on the side of fear was death. I clearly had to make a choice because faith and fear cannot coexist. One had to completely go and the choice was mine. With the help of the Holy Spirit, I chose faith, and I began a journey of choosing faith over fear.

I tell you this story because the Spurs came alongside me and walked beside me, held me, and prayed for this precious child for at least twenty-five years. In fact, they have never stopped praying. Even though the battle for this one is not over, we still choose faith.

My verse, my "holding on " verse is from 2 Timothy 1:12 (KJV).

....for I know whom I have believed, and am persuaded that he is able to keep that which I have committed unto Him against that day.

God has not only redeemed this child but is in the process of setting her free. In the meantime, He is continually setting me free.

A Time to Redeem

A powerful love that can redeem anything.

by Pat Reynolds

......the kingdom of heaven suffers violence,
and the violent take it by force.
Matthew 11:12 (NKJV)

The Spurs have become my sisters who walk with me through victories, pains and sorrows. Their connectedness to me has brought family, comfort, strength and hope. Our prayers and sharing together through the years has been a directional wind for my spiritual sails, but there came a time when my sails were torn and ripped apart. The wind of the Spurs carried me. For several years, I could not read the Bible or pray. I was in God's ICU.

The God who has established a natural order allows out-of-order events: miracles and tragedies. It is out of order for children to die before their parents. There are now five Spur children who have entered into the main event—"God's Heavenly Presence." All five had been soaked with prayer throughout the years of the Spurs' existence, prayers for victory, release and healing. Our daughter, Andrea, was the first and youngest of the Spur children to die. She was twenty years old.

The jolting call came at 1:30 a.m. from the emergency room at the hospital in San Marcos, Texas.

"Your daughter is in ICU with multiple gunshot wounds."

We prayed.

The second call came at 1:45 a.m.
  "Your daughter is dead. Her boyfriend, Scott, has been shot
  thirteen times.
  He is alive and in surgery."
We prayed.

Around 4:00 a.m. Scott died during surgery.
We prayed, cried, prayed, cried.

My friend Maria came to us early that morning, and comforted us and prayed with us. Maria and I have been close spiritually and professionally. She helped Andrea through some troubled times and has been a source of strength and encouragement to our family through the years. She helped shoulder the pain we were feeling.

The next faces I remember were three Spurs—Gayle, Molly, and Carolyn. One of them asked me, "How are you?" I replied, "I feel naked, covered with dung." This was the beginning of the supply of strength the Spurs would provide for me throughout the years after Andrea's death. God's forceful love through the Spurs helped me on my journey. My long history with them has provided a consistent and smooth support for the path I walk.

Andrea and Scott had gone to visit a friend in college. The friend, Susie, had broken up that day with her live-in boyfriend, Joe. Joe was distraught. He began drinking, taking Prozac and LSD. By the time Andrea and Scott got there shortly after midnight he was violent and incoherent, hallucinating from the LSD. Soon after they arrived, they called for an ambulance for him.

Then Susie started to call Joe's brother and Joe jerked the phone out of her hand. Scott then pinned Joe against the wall saying, "You can't treat a girl that way." Joe grabbed his semi-automatic rifle that was hanging on the wall above him and shot all fifty rounds, showering the apartment. Scott fell over Susie, shielding her from the spray of bullets. Only one bullet nicked her neck. She was seen in the emergency room and released. Andrea had been hit three times, and one of the bullets had severed her aorta. She probably died within three minutes. She was dead when we got the first call.

Two lived: the murderer and his ex-girlfriend.

Two died: Our daughter and her boyfriend.

Why? Why my daughter? How sufficient is God's grace? Sheldon Vanauken, in *A Severe Mercy,* asks how a loving God could allow his beloved young wife Davy to die. What is the purpose and meaning in God's sovereignty? His friend C. S. Lewis responded, "Christ must often seem to us to be playing fast and loose with us. The adult must seem to mislead the child and the Master the dog. They misread the signs. Their ignorance and their wishes twist everything. You are so sure you know what the promise promised."

A month before her death, I had been moved by the scripture "The Kingdom of Heaven suffers violence and the violent take it by force" (Matthew 11:12 NKJV).

My child would suffer violence (she was a child of the Kingdom of God) but even with that violence, I would come to experience a greater force than murder: the love of God. Even the intensity in my prayer time was an example of the spirit grieving the suffering and terrible things that happen to God's children in this fallen world. We all have physical death, a faith shaker for earthlings. We would like to design the time, process and place of our death, but the only design we have is choosing eternal life through Christ Jesus and maybe our earthly burial plot. Our time is in God's hands. (Psalm 31:15.)

The last three weeks before Andrea's death, she had visited friends. She took her niece and nephew to Six Flags. She was home for the summer taking courses at a junior college. Our relationship was the best it had ever been. I so wanted it to last for me until I got rid of this earthly suit. It was as though she had some deep sense of needing to say goodbye to everyone she loved.

Three days before Andrea's murder, I had such a powerful sense of prayer that all I wanted to do was pray night and day. It was like the Holy Spirit was praying through my spirit with a grieving that cannot be expressed in words. The apostle Paul prayed at times when it was so deep that words could not be uttered, only groaning. (Romans 8:26-27 NKJV.)

I wanted to spend time praying but I had set up a time to play tennis at Sally Renshaw's house, who is a Spur. I brought with me the minister's wife Betsi from our church. A Spurs' son, Jeff Davis, made up the foursome. I did not realize that the beginning of the funeral plans had started. As Betsi and I rode to Sally's, we talked about hymns we liked (which I ended up using at the funeral). Betsi's husband, Tim, officiated at the funeral.

During the three-day period prior to Andrea's death, my praying centered on the woman who "begged" Jesus to heal her daughter. Her great faith statement was that "even the dogs eat the crumbs that fall from the master's table" (Matthew 15:27). At the time, I thought I was interceding for my older daughter, Grace, not realizing the prayer was for Andrea.

In God's kindness, He did prepare the way for this devastating goodbye. I could not have prayed any more than I did. The last time I saw Andrea, she had come from a friend's house about 1:30 a.m. I was up reading the Bible and praying. One of her last comments to me was: "I might know you would be up praying." She said this with affection and warmth. Unknown to both of us was the reason I so diligently prayed. In twenty-four hours she would be gone.

Prior to this, in the past few years, I would go to St. Patrick's Catholic Church in Dallas to pray, even though I am not Catholic. The church was open all day. St. Patrick's is not an ornate church. Architecturally it is more modern with simple lines. I love the large figure of the resurrected Jesus hanging above the altar. His wide-open arms enveloped the whole room. I would do the Stations of the Cross, which portray the last hours of Jesus' life before His resurrection. They depict the agony on the way to the cross and on the cross. The last station is Him painfully crucified. Then you look up at the huge figure on the wall. HE HAS RISEN!

The Protestant picture of this figure for me is: He is ascending into Heaven to be with the Father yet His heart and care still remain with us on earth. I would sit and look at this risen Jesus and meditate. The large windows on the east and west guaranteed tremendous light and shadows on the figure of Jesus.

The day of Andrea's funeral was the toughest day of my life. There was no escape from the reality of her death. I couldn't do it. In order to get strength for the funeral service, in this state of desperation, I went to my place of solace and comfort: St. Patrick's Church. As I fell on my knees, I could not speak; the violence and pain in my world had overcome me (Psalm 61:1-4). Andrea would be gone forever in this life. I knew God the Father had let go of His Son, and Mary, the mother of Jesus, let go of her murdered Son. Now in a lesser measure, I had joined their ranks. Yet I didn't want to join their ranks. I didn't want this kind of suffering and loss. As I looked up to Jesus, I began to experience His intense love for me, for Andrea, for her killer, and for the whole world. The intensity of this love was flooding through my being. It was so overwhelming! I could not have stood it for too long. It literally was an energy that vibrated my physical body. I had to brace myself so I would not fall, even though I was not standing up. Overwhelming pain demands overwhelming love. (Psalm 18:1-6.)

As the intensity waned, I began to have double vision. The figure of Jesus was remaining on the wall and yet He was floating down, putting His arms around me. In these moments I had transcended the pain and the ravaging loss of Andrea. I was engulfed in His presence. In that glory moment there was no sorrow or pain. My loss was not a loss. This violent force of love had more power and intensity than Andrea's violent murder. Did I stay in that strong feeling moment? No. It became a "powerful feeling memory" that helped to sustain me as I journeyed through the path of pain. (Psalm 18:16-19.)

My friend Maria came to St. Patrick's to help and support me through this dark, dismal day. With the experience I had at St. Patrick's, Maria's help, and the support of the Spurs and others, I was enabled to go through the unwanted day of the funeral.

It is now almost twenty years since Andrea's murder. What has been the learning, changing outcome of this tragedy for me? Here are some conclusions:

- What happened to her will never be okay.

- I miss her earthly existence and promise.

- All those involved in her life and murder are fully forgiven.

- "This place is not my home. I am just passing through"— (a gospel song). (1 Peter 1:17-21.)

- I have peace and hope and I can't wait to see her.

- The force of God's love produces a violence (force) in us that overcomes the violence of the world.

- God's plan for our journey is to be in community with other believers.

- This life is not the main event—only a staging place for the everlasting joy that is set before me.

I read "the talk" in Job, where

The Lord answered Job from the whirlwind:
    Job 38:1 (NLT)

Brace yourself like a man because I have some questions for you, and you must answer them.
    Job 38:3 (NLT)

As Job listens, God instructs him on how limited is his knowledge and understanding. See Job 38 through 41. Now Job answers:

I have only heard about you before.
Now I have seen you with my own eyes"
  Job 42:5-6 (NLT)

Job had believed in the Lord already, but now he clearly understood that he could not understand the Lord's ways (Job 42:3,6). The decisions of the Creator, God of the universe, cannot be grasped or understood. In regard to what happened to Andrea, I clearly understand that I don't understand. I clearly understand that I can't understand. (Colossians 1:15-20)

Job never knew the "why" of what happened to him. I don't know "why" God allowed Andrea's murder. God has not chosen to prevent all evil from happening in this world for reasons I don't understand, but He has chosen to give sufficient and abundant help in our pain and needs. In this mysterious relationship with the Lord, I only understand Him in a limited way, but He understands me fully.

Did God answer the Spurs' prayers for Andrea's victory and healing? You need to ask Andrea. Have I had fullness of life after her death? You need to ask me. Do I on occasions still have a momentary rush of sadness and loss? Yes, but I don't have a chronic sorrow that robs me of life.

The force and violence of God's love for me, through my family, the Spurs and friends, are greater than death, murder, abuse, suicide—anything!

Place me like a seal over your heart, like a seal on your arm.
For love is as strong as death, its jealousy as enduring as
the grave. Love flashes like fire, the brightest kind of flame.
Many waters cannot quench love, nor can rivers drown it. If
a man tried to buy love with all his wealth, his offer would
be utterly scorned.
  Song of Songs 8:6-7 (NLT)

About two or three months after Andrea's death, I had a dream. In the dream, I found myself at the train station. As I looked around, I saw Andrea walking toward me with a tremendous glow on her face. She was radiant. I had never seen her looking so happy. The scene reminded me of seeing your daughter off for an exciting, adventurous trip.

She was excited but I was not. I didn't want her to go. As she came closer, I said, "Andrea, don't go!" As I looked into her face, I saw her compassion and understanding for my feelings about her leaving. Like a parent talking to a child, she reassured me that she loved me and everything would be okay, but she must go. She wanted to go where she was going. In the distance, I could hear and see two girls calling "Andrea, get on the train. Hurry up. It's about to leave!" The train whistle was blowing; the conductor was loudly announcing "All aboard! All aboard!" I still pleaded with her not to go as she slipped through my arms. She had swiftly walked toward me; now she was swiftly walking away. She boarded the train. She didn't look back. She was gone. I will never forget her radiant and loving face.

"Rise up, my darling!
Come away with me, my fair one!
Look, the winter is past, and the rains are over and gone.
The flowers are springing up, the season of singing birds has come, and the cooing of turtledoves fills the air.
The fig trees are forming young fruit, and the fragrant grapevines are blossoming.
Rise up, my darling!
Come away with me, my fair one!"
Song of Songs 2:10-13 (NLT)

Pat Reynolds *(center)*, four generations in 1990.
Left to right standing: Daughters Andrea and Grace.
Left to right seated: Granddaughter Hannah and mother Mary Geis.

A Time for Mercy
Sentencing for the Accused
by Pat Reynolds

His mercy endures forever.
Psalm 138:8 (NKJV)

*T*buried Andrea in July 1991.
I buried my mother the following February.

In March, I attended the sentencing of Joe, the young man who murdered my daughter. He pleaded guilty, and it was now time for justice to be served through sentencing.

In the tiny courtroom in San Marcos, Texas, were my husband Bob, my children Grace and John, and my Spur friends Molly Dummit and Ann Hyde. Joe's parents were half an arm's length in front of me. I could touch them with my breath. In addition there were Joe's four siblings. Andrea's boyfriend Scott's family was sitting to my right at the end of the bench, but there were no siblings for Scott, as he was an only child. Scott's uncle was a Baylor Law School graduate. His grandfather had been Dean of Baylor Law School, then later, President of Baylor University. The prosecuting attorney and maybe the presiding judge had graduated from Baylor Law School. This added another element of pressure to the courtroom procedures. There we were, cramped together—three sets of bewildered, brokenhearted parents, and six bewildered, brokenhearted siblings. Possibly all were believers from different Christian traditions.

During a court recess, I came face to face with Joe's parents in the hall. I remember telling them that God's love was stronger than death, and stronger than murder. As I spoke to them, they had a frozen pain on their face. I don't remember if they replied or not. I knew I could be standing in their shoes. My children could have easily driven a car under the influence of alcohol and caused a death. I would need mercy. My child would need mercy. If that had happened to us, we would have hoped for and needed mercy. Now these parents needed mercy. Their son needed mercy. Mercy's end is redemption. (Titus 3:4-7)

The court proceeding was like a mini trial in which different people gave testimony to help the judge determine a just sentence. Scott's mother, my husband Bob and daughter Grace gave testimony. Joe's mother, father and elder brother gave testimony on his behalf. Sue, Joe's ex-girlfriend who was wounded but lucid during the shooting episode, gave an account of what happened. Joe's counselor testified for him. I chose not to give testimony to that which I thought was so obvious: the price we already had paid and will continue to pay for losing our daughter.

Under Texas Law, Joe could have received the death penalty. This was one decision we had to make—whether to support that possibility or not. Bob wrote a letter to the judge and prosecutor making request for prison time only. Since the crime was committed when Joe was hallucinating on LSD, and there was not premeditated intent, we felt the death penalty was not appropriate for him.

Joe was a junior in college majoring in psychology. Joe's young counselor, who worked at the college, portrayed him as caring and sensitive. She recommended a short sentence, then probation, giving community service to help others. Her youthful idealistic belief in change had no roots to it. Her psychology would not have the powerful mercy that can change your heart and release you from what you have done. (Isaiah 52:7, 61:1)

The combined testimonies for Joe revealed a sensitive, insecure and troubled young man. The mother was more justifying of Joe's sensitivities and weaknesses while the father wanted him to toughen up (guns and hunting). In that quick glimpse of their situation, I could see there was trouble between them over Joe. Tragedies break fragile relationships.

The prosecuting attorney met with my family and reviewed the case. He wanted to make sure he could get the verbal evidence and testimonies that could insure a long sentence. I had very little interest in the evidence or the legal procedure. I was merely adhering to "the laws of the land"—the earthly legal system for lawlessness. All I remember about his sentence is that Joe was given two fifteen-year sentences, and he had to serve fifteen years before he was eligible for parole. He has since had his fifteen-year parole hearing but was denied parole. When a person comes up for a parole hearing, the parole system of Texas will send a notification to the family of the pending parole meeting. The parole board will consider the letters from family as a part of their decision-making. Bob and I did not write letters to influence the parole board. We had released and trusted Joe's consequences to God.

As I sat in the courtroom, my feelings moved from numb to pain back to numb. At times, I felt that I was observing a scene in a play where I did not have a part. However, I must be a reluctant participant in "justice" being done. I have seen people on television state that they can finally be at rest or get freedom to get on with living when "justice" has been done.

Earthly justice for Joe murdering my daughter did not give me rest or release me to get on with my life. My meaning for life comes from the inside life I have with Jesus. At times, that life with Jesus is stronger. There are other times that life is weaker.

Because this was a homicide case, both Andrea and Scott had to have a toxicology report. The report cleared them of drugs and alcohol in the blood. The conclusion of the police report is that Scott and Andrea were in the wrong place at the wrong time. I, however, believe there are no wrong places or wrong times within the sovereignty of God.

When this terrible event happened, Bob and I each had a history of a relationship with God. I had had my faith struggle in my early thirties. In that struggle, I moved from anger, to disbelief, to unbelief about God and His existence. Being in a dark place of unbelief about God's existence brought me the most pain I had ever experienced prior to Andrea's death. In Andrea's death there was comfort, the warmth of God's love and compassion. I have a future hope of seeing Andrea again. In the darkness of my rebellion and unbelief, there was no comfort, no hope—only desolation. Thankfully, God brought me to *His* senses through kindness and mercy. In the midst of my deepest anger and unbelief, He gifted me with my first pregnancy, Andrea. The fertility specialist had said that pregnancy would be impossible for Bob and me.

I have come to know a Holy Father that is good and caring, though He could have, but did not, circumvent Andrea's and Scott's deaths. (Psalm 31:19-20)

My children didn't have my long history with the Father. Grace was twenty-nine and John was eighteen when Andrea was murdered. How would I convey to them that God is good, loving and caring? I couldn't. I would need to learn patience and wait for the Father's redemptive timing for them. (Psalm 44:2-4) It took a long time, so I needed the Spurs for a long time. They helped me be refreshed with the truth and strengthened me with their love. Their belief in the Jesus in me kept me from fainting. The Spurs have been guardrails for me on this unknown journey. (Jude 1:20-21) They have provided a constant community for me whether I am weak or strong.

I also leaned heavily on my past mentors: Dietrich Bonhoeffer (*The Cost of Discipleship*) and Viktor Frankl (*Man's Search for Meaning*). They helped to provide reins to my heart and a way of seeing a bigger picture than my circumstances. Both men had experienced the atrocities of Nazi Germany in World War II: Bonhoeffer, an evangelical Lutheran, and Frankl, a Jew. Bonhoeffer was in England at the time of the war with Germany. He made a deliberate decision to go back to Germany to be an encouragement to his Lutheran brethren who were suffering at the hands of the Nazis. Acting against the protests of believers, he went, knowing his death might be imminent. He chose to lay down his physical life in order to live out his spiritual belief. (Revelation 12:11) He wrote a poem in prison, *Who am I*. Suffering can distort and play havoc with your identity. The last line in his poem states,

"Whoever I am, thou knowest, O God, I am thine." Bonhoeffer died by special order of Gestapo deputy director Himmler, three days before Allied forces liberated his prison.

There is no cheap grace. Living in grace and giving grace will cost you. It cost Jesus His life. T.S. Eliot in *The Four Quartets* says what it is to be a Christian: "A condition of complete simplicity (costing not less than everything)." To give grace to the murderer of your daughter costs. (Micah 6:8)

Frankl lived but lost his beloved bride and family. Frankl was a young, newly married, Viennese psychiatrist when he was sent to Auschwitz, the Polish concentration camp. In the shuddering cold of Polish winters with an ever-present hunger in his guts, Frankl had to endure the added humiliation of jesting Nazi soldiers sloshing him with the latrines' refuse. Through this inhumane treatment and trauma, he discovered the real source of strength to stay alive. Real life was not an outer experience but an inner experience. He who has a "why" to live can bear with almost any "how." What you believe, think and hope has a greater power for giving you living reality than your circumstances. He realized suffering has meaning. It can produce understanding and deep knowing. Jesus suffered in order to learn obedience. (Hebrews 5:8) Deep truth and understanding can overtake your circumstances. The New Testament version of Frankl's truth would be: a seed must die, drop to the ground, and then it brings forth new life. Suffering and death to self is the process of new life (resurrection): so that we may know Jesus in the power of His resurrection and the fellowship of His suffering. (Philippians 3:10) Suffering and resurrection are co-equal truths.

I absolutely believe that wrongful acts need consequences; however, earthly justice does not heal or free you. It is Jesus' mercy that heals and frees you. Did Joe's sentencing, incarceration, or even his apparent lack of remorse make a difference to me? Not really. The puritan writer Watson said, "God's judgment drips but His mercy flows." I want mercy for Joe, myself and others. (Jude 1:22-23) God's mercy has discipline and correction. The end of God's mercy is to draw us to Himself so He can erase our wrongs and failures with redemptive love and freedom.

Suffering has meaning. It awakens us to truth and helps us to have endurance and understanding. The suffering over Andrea's death has helped me clarify my bottom line. My bottom line to love God is foremost. God's love processed through me and you will cost. Learning to trust and obey will necessitate suffering. (1 Peter 1:6-8, 13-14)

Everlasting life is everlasting! All our life's experiences are infused with mercy that turns our hearts to the Sun of Righteousness (Malachi 4:2) who has healing in His Wings! The Sun of Righteousness, Christ Jesus, tells us to fear not. His hand is upon us. He is alive and He is the conqueror. (Revelation 1:14-18) God's mercy endures forever!

Pat Reynolds

A Time to Reflect

from Pat and Bob Reynolds

September 2, 1991

Dear Friends,

*T*his letter is to express our appreciation and love to all of you who have supported us in so many ways since the death of our daughter Andrea.

We loved Andrea. We love all our children in their own special uniqueness. They each add something to our lives that no one else can. We see ourselves in each of them in a special way, and that is one reason the loss of a child is so great. A part of us is taken, and a part of our future.

God let us have Andrea for twenty years. We have many fond memories of her to keep. She went with us on a vacation trip to Arizona for a week during her spring break in March, and we had a great time. We went to Carlsbad Caverns, stayed with some friends in Sedona, Arizona, and saw the Grand Canyon. Bob and Andrea took a helicopter ride over the canyon.

Andrea lived in Waco the last two years, but this summer she was here with us going to Richland College. Bob tutored her in her math course, and helped her plan her future goals since she wanted to transfer to a four-year college in the fall. Pat spent a lot of time fellowshipping with her—helping with her speeches for speech class, buying clothes, and talking about the issues of life.

We reinforced many close ties with Andrea during this summer. We are grateful that God allowed us to have this time together.

We will especially remember Andrea's unique sense of humor. She had an ear for words and sounds, and would always laugh at a deliberate mispronunciation such as "aminals" for "animals," or Archie Bunker-type substitutions of similar sounding but erroneous words. Bob frequently wrote limericks and other doggerel for her, which she always appreciated, and she would laugh with Pat over funny things they experienced.

Andrea was a sensitive and caring person who had had her share of life's sorrows. She had walked both in the valleys and on the mountaintops. She loved animals and considered majoring in biology so she could work in a zoo. She identified with the underdog and could relate to a wide variety of people. More than one teenager has come to us, broken over her death, and said that Andrea was the best friend they ever had.

She was in a developing and growing phase of life in which she was experiencing the satisfaction of success that comes when new challenges are undertaken and goals are met. While in Waco she had obtained her GED and then gone on to McLennan Community College. Later, she realized the importance of the high school diploma and the loss of not having it. She went back to high school in Waco and completed her courses during the fall semester of last year. They were transferred back to Lake Highlands High School and she graduated from there this spring with our son John. She was very proud of herself, and we were proud of her for her accomplishment.

Andrea knew the Lord Jesus as her Savior. She accepted Him at an early age, and later affirmed her faith to others on several occasions. We received two cards from friends who had personal knowledge of Andrea's faith, and these were a great source of comfort to us. Her spiritual life was just in the budding stage, but we could see indications of her basic spiritual nature and were confident that she would continue to progress into spiritual maturity as God led her along.

The loss of Andrea leaves a big empty place in our lives. While we have experienced the comfort of friends and of the Holy Spirit, we realize that her unique contribution to our lives is irreplace-able. It is a loss, and it will always be a loss. But God is faithful; He does not ask us to walk a path that he does not guide us in, or carry a load that He does not strengthen us for. If afflicted in every way, we are not crushed; if perplexed, we are not despairing; if persecuted, we are not forsaken; if struck down, we are not destroyed. (2 Cor. 4:18) "Therefore we do not lose heart, but though our outer man is decaying, yet our inner man is being renewed day by day. For momentary, light affliction is producing for us an eternal weight of glory far beyond all comparison, while we look not at the things which are seen, but at the things which are not seen; for the things which are seen are temporal, but the things which are not seen are eternal." (2 Cor. 4:16-18)

It is a great comfort to know that, even though our earthly family has been decreased by one, there is a corresponding family in Heaven that has now been increased by one. Andrea is the first to make the transition, but we shall see her again. "For we have a building from God, a house not made with hands, eternal in the heavens. For indeed in this house we groan, longing to be clothed with our dwelling from heaven. For indeed while we are in this tent, we groan, being burdened, because we do not want to be swallowed up by life. Now He who prepared us for this very pur-pose is God, who gave us the Spirit as a pledge. Therefore being always of good courage, and knowing that while we are at home in the body we are absent from the Lord—for we walk by faith, not by sight—we are of good courage, I say, and prefer rather to be absent from the body and to be at home with the Lord. Therefore also we have as our ambition, whether at home or absent, to be pleasing to Him." (2 Cor. 5:1-2, 4-9)

We are not angry with God. There is a time for all things, a time to live and a time to die. Someone has correctly said that God does not save us from trouble; He saves us from our sins, and enables us to get through trouble. Andrea's death was out of the normal order of events, but for some reason, which is hidden from us, God in His providence chose her to be the first to see Him. We do not feel compelled to know the answers for this loss. It would be a futile search, for God seldom reveals such things in this life. It must be a matter of faith, a confidence that the God who has done so much for us does all things well, and this event is not an exception. We see in a very limited sense, while God stands over time and eternity and sees the end from the beginning. Why should it surprise us that we do not understand all His ways?

We are still hurting, but we are healing. God does not want us to labor under grief forever. He is a God who heals, who does exceeding abundantly above all that we could ask or think. And we cannot overemphasize to each one of you who receive this letter how much we appreciate the part you have played in ministering this healing to us.

To those who called to express your sympathy and love, we say thanks.

To those who visited us, thank you.

To those who sent cards and letters expressing your feelings for us, thank you.

To those who brought food and supplies, we are grateful.

To those who spent many hours at our home preparing food, cleaning up, answering the phone, and doing whatever was needed to help us out, our heartfelt thanks.

To those who sent flowers, we appreciate it, and enjoyed them very much.

To those who could take out the time to attend the memorial service, we appreciate you.

To those who made yourselves available to help out if needed, we thank you.

To the many, many who have prayed for us during this time, we are grateful.

To those who contributed to the Matthew Foundation or contributed Gideon Bibles as a memorial, we thank you.

To those who gave special attention to our son, John, and our daughter, Grace, we thank you.

To all of you who contributed gifts and expressions of love, thank you.

We have never had to deal with a tragic event such as this, and therefore did not realize how important the love and care of friends really are. We realize it now; your outpouring to us has been a true blessing, and has helped us greatly. May the Lord in return shower His blessings upon you.

Even so, come Lord Jesus, come quickly. Amen.

Bob and Pat Reynolds

A Time to Rest

by Pat Reynolds

My soul finds rest in God alone;....
Psalm 62:1
How can we sing the songs of the LORD while in a foreign land?
Psalm 137:4

September 2001

My dearest Spurs,

The summer of 2001 marked a decade, or ten years, since our daughter Andrea's murder. Bob and I have found a place of peace and rest regarding this tragic event. That's not saying that on occasion we don't experience sorrow, because we do. But this sorrow does not limit or define our relationship to God, others, and ourselves. I can even say that I have experienced spiritual benefits from this awful event. Just to mention one: in Russia, one out of four people have been murdered, particularly in World War II and during Stalin's years of reign. In World War II, the Germans surrounded St. Petersburg for 900 days, cutting off food supplies, which resulted in a third of the city starving. My loss puts me in a similar boat with the Russians. While in Russia, I did not promote my story of Andrea as an entrance point, but only when asked or when it was an appropriate avenue to lock into my deepest story, which is my relationship with Jesus and being a conduit of God's grace. Experiences don't always have to be spoken because spirit-to-spirit speaks the loudest.

I am writing about this because I have a present story that probably includes all of us with our children, our grandchildren, or ourselves. I took my daughter Grace to the "Women of Faith" conference. After the woman who was raped, tortured, but not killed by the character in "Dead Man Walking" gave her testimony of God's grace and healing, plus her forgiveness, Grace began to cry and told about Andrea's death. Our children can get stuck, struggling with a "loving God, who cares for His children," but allows awful things to happen. Our children become vagrants, sometimes even prodigals, in a distant land.

A vagrant is one who does not have a settled home. People cannot truly rest until they find their rest in God. I know that I am not alone regarding children or grandchildren who have not had a homecoming in an area of their lives. There cannot be a home-coming when we judge God's character and ways, and refuse or become afraid to trust Him in any revealed area of our lives He wants to touch. We want to understand about situations that do not make sense or seem unfair. When we cannot, we become stuck or unsettled.

So through the years, I hear, I say, I experience the "unset-tledness" of our children, now grandchildren; looking back but not seeing, hunting but not finding, as they go here and there searching for peace and rest. I know that our children need to have their own process time, but I feel some of our children have wandered long enough. I know as a mother you can't usually have a direct hit, so you manipulate. Now what got my idea going is that Grace wanted to be more a part of the Spurs. So when I said, "Would you like to get with the Spurs for a mother-daughter deal?" she grabbed it.

At our Mother-Daughter "Settling In" weekends we have had:

1. Fun—games, skits, Molly's jokes, laughter;
2. Focus—telling Stories of the Spurs (SOS);

3. Fusion—reconciliations with God, others, and self from the unending giving of God's grace;
4. Friendship—thanksgiving and forgiving.

G — **G**race
I — **I**nvites
V — **V**agrants (those who have not come home yet, and those who are unsettled)
E — **E**xclusively selected, picked, elected, called.

Grace invites vagrants exclusively.

Having received your many tender mercies and kindnesses, I give to you tender mercies and kindness.

Pat

Spurred by Grace
Chapter Eleven

A Time for Celebrations

A Time for a Mother-Daughter Dinner

by Kathleen Page Clark

*They devoted themselves to the apostles' teaching
and to the fellowship,
to the breaking of bread and to prayer.
Acts 2:42*

The Spurs and their daughters and daughters-in-law gathered for the first time at the Shady Oaks Country Club in Fort Worth, Texas, on March 11, 1999. It was a delightful and memorable evening. The daughters told stories about their mothers that many of the Spurs had never heard before. There was much laughter! There was also bonding that took place among the daughters and daughters-in-law that remains to this day.

Not all the Spurs nor all of their daughters or daughters-in-law were there. Those who could not attend, regret it. Those who could attend, cherish the memories.

Here is a sampling of the smiling faces!

Left to right: Daughter Debbie, Carolyn Boyd, daughter Karan.

Left to right: Daughter-in-law Tisha, daughter Kathleen, Mary Alice Brumley.

Left to right standing: Daughters Alaine, Dayna, Susan with Barbara Clarkin.
Left to right kneeling: Daughter-in-laws Dianne, Karen and Julie.

Left to right: Daughter-in-law Karen Eagan, daughter Caren Slaton, Maureen Eagan.

Left to right: Daughter Annie Laurie and Anne Hyde.

Left to right: Daughter Kristi and Mimi Mack

Left to right: Sally Renshaw and daughter Julie.

Left to right: Daughter Grace and Pat Reynolds.

Left to right: Daughter Kathy, Mary Jo Scheideman,
daughters-in-law Sara and Margaret.

Left to right: Janet Sheats, daughter-in-law Trish
and Trish's mother Patsy.

Left to right: Daughters-in-law Tracy, Cindy,
Georgia Smith, daughter-in-law Amy.

Left to right: Daughter-in-law Jennifer with Sandra Talkington.

Left to right: Harriet Wallace with daughter-in-law Mary Evelyn.

A Time for a Mother-Daughter Retreat

by Kathleen Page Clark

Our mouths were filled with laughter,
our tongues with songs of joy....
Psalm 126:2

The Spurs and their daughters and daughters-in-law had such fond memories of their dinner three years earlier that they wanted to do something together again. This time we gathered for a weekend retreat at a local hotel near the Dallas/Ft Worth airport on February 1-3, 2002. We wanted the next generation of Spurs to get to know each other more or for the first time. We have prayed, and continue to pray, for each of them through the years. We wanted to finally put names to faces. We also wanted them to get to know us.

We planned a fun get-acquainted game. Little did we know how fun and funny it would be!

Each Spur was asked to submit three facts about themselves that was a part of their mysterious past. We were encouraged to think of things that even our own daughters and daughters-in-law might not know about us. We had an unexpected surprise! Little did we know that we would find out a lot about each other that we did not know, even though we had been together as a group for decades.

All the Spurs sat in chairs, side-by-side, on one side of the room. We then had all the daughters and daughters-in-law sit side-by-side across the room from us, so we could face each other.

I cut the statements that each Spur had given me into strips of paper and mixed them all up in a paper sack. I read each fact, one at a time, and the daughters and daughters-in-law were to try to guess as a group who belonged to which fact. Can you imagine the laughter?

The amazing thing that occurred is that the daughters and daughters-in-law continually picked Georgia to match many, many more than three facts! Georgia was the eldest Spur and at that time was in her late seventies. Way to go, Georgia! Keep them guessing!

Just to give you a picture of the rich history and diversity that each Spur brings to the group, we thought it would be fun to include the list in this book. Needless to say, we are not identifying the Spurs who claim such interesting pasts—especially the nudist!

I will give you a clue, however. The group of three statements listed together is from the same Spur. If you can guess one, you might learn two little known facts about that same person!

Enjoy!

I took piano lessons from the time I was five years old through the twelfth grade.
If I would go back to college today, I would like to major in business.
We lived in North Dakota for two years.

I was a football queen in high school.
I rode a bicycle to class every day when I was a student at Stanford University.
My family was the first largest family to ever fly on American Airlines. We flew on a DC9 to Washington DC in the late forties.

My pet squirrel (Happy Jack) was one of the first animals
to fly in an open cockpit plane.
I was a navigator in an airplane for twelve years.
I am a daughter of the American Revolution: fifth generation of fighting with George Washington.

I was the County Spelling Bee Champion in the eighth
grade.
I was Queen of the SWAAU Basketball Tournament in
Duncanville in 1959.
I do stained glass.

When I was first born, my parents named me Lois Virginia.
I graduated from high school when I was sixteen and three
months.
I have helicoptered over the continental divide.

I made All-State choir in high school.
During the eighth month of my first pregnancy, my house
blew over—with me in it!
The beginning to my tennis enthusiasm started in high
school when never having hit a tennis ball, I entered a
park tournament with a friend and we won first place.
(No one else showed up for the doubles matches).

I weighed over nine pounds when I was born.
I won a scholarship to college from the local Rotary Club
in Columbus, Ohio.
I want to be a flute-playing ballerina in my next life.

I once played Beethoven's Sonata Pathétique.
I once was a Republican precinct chairman.
I once lived in Fort Wayne, Indiana.

I was awarded the Blue Ribbon for first place in a horse show.
I went on a Texas Tour with a Gilbert and Sullivan operetta.
I sang in La Boehme opera (chorus).

I became a Christian at thirty—a late bloomer.
I have walked on the Great Wall of China.
I was a "Mermaid" at the University of Arizona water ballet team. Yes, Esther Williams was my hero.

I would rather work outside than inside any day.
I turned down a scholarship to study in England.
My first college major was Speech and TV, but I was replaced because I kept getting tickled. Needless to say, I changed my major.

In grammar school, I could stand on my head longer than anyone else.
I was a Cotton Bowl queen in the '50s.
I was on Dave Garroway's Today Show, Steve Allen's Tonight Show and Break the Bank in 1955.

I have Elvis Presley's autograph.
I beat Tony Dorsett, the Dallas Cowboy running back, in a short running race.
As a child, I was an excellent fly fisherman (or fisherwoman).

I speak Hebrew.
I almost died in Greece.
I am a former "Little Miss Lutz/Land-O-Lakes."

I taught a Bible study at Bauder Beauty College.
My grandmother lived on a plantation.
I designed and made needlepoint canvases.

I learned to play the piano at an early age so that I could accompany my father, who was an opera singer.

I studied at the University of Chicago.

I went caving and floating down the river with ten other nude teenage girls at a camp for John Brown University.

In my youth, I could bend my fingers back to almost touch my wrist.

My husband was a hell raiser and a half before I led him to Christ.

I have performed before state governors.

When I was four years old, while my mother was having all of our relatives to our home for Easter, I took my two-year-old brother under the bed and cut his hair.

A boy in high school, after our first date, went home and told his mother that he had met the girl he was going to marry—and he did!

My sixth grade boyfriend sang the song "Trees" on the school program and dedicated it to me.

I have a velveteen rabbit that goes wherever I go.

(Note: This Spur was too embarrassed by her other two facts so she requested they be deleted.)

Oh, Spurs! Let's do this again soon! I easily have three more statements about myself that no one will guess!

A Time for Birthdays
for Georgia Smith
by Kathleen Page (Elliott) Clark

.....a time to be born and a time to die.....
Ecclesiastes 3:2

*B*irthdays are a special time to honor and celebrate each other. With the Spurs, often on decade changes, a poem is written for that special person. When our eldest Spur turned eighty years old in 2008, this is the poem I wrote and read to Georgia Smith. It captured our love for her.

Happy Eightieth Birthday, Georgia!

Happy Birthday, Georgia! I'm glad we're all here
To gather and celebrate your eightieth year.
We honor you now as our eldest Spur
Your youthful spirit makes age just a blur.

Georgia, my dear, you amaze me so!
I don't think you know the meaning of "slow."
Your energy never seems to end
But your greatest gift is that of a friend.

I fell in love with you when we first met.
Our time in Missouri, I will NEVER forget!
You did us a cheer that was OH so good
But once on your knees, you remained, not stood!

Your laughter's contagious and lights up your face.
And also you always are so full of grace.
Your hospitality is WAY above par.
We drive west to your home, no matter how far.

I love you, Georgia! I hope you know.
Each year that love continues to grow.
Not many octogenarians do as you do.
I want to grow up to be JUST like you!

Love, hugs and birthday blessings!
Kathleen Page Elliott
February 3, 2008

Georgia Smith doing a high school cheer! "How do I get up?"

A Time for the Joy of Christmas
Joy to the World! The Lord has come!
by Mary Jo Scheideman

He will be a joy and delight to you,
and many will rejoice because of his birth....
Luke 1:14

*O*h, the delight of gathering together at Christmas to celebrate the source of our joy: the birth of our Lord and Savior, Jesus Christ.

The Scheideman's crèche.

I have had the privilege of hosting the Spurs annual Christmas party for many years. My health keeps me from attending many of the day meetings, so I especially look forward to having them all gather in my home each year in early December. Their presence is one of the many anticipated joys of the season. This has become a very meaningful tradition.

The Spurs gather in the Scheideman living room
for the angel gift exchange. December 2011.

Carol Williams is a wonderful Spur musician. We often gather around our grand piano in the living room as she plays and we all sing Christmas carols. We are all of the age when this used to be done in homes more often than is done now, so this is a special time. Many of the Spurs have beautiful voices, which makes us sound really good!

A delicious lunch is always catered, unlike most gatherings when everyone brings a salad or dessert. Instead of bringing food, we each bring a wrapped Christmas angel to exchange. Some have wrapped the angels in gilded boxes and large gift bags to entice and tempt us to choose just the right one. We are each given a number, and in that ascending order, each person either selects a new package or "steals" one that is already opened. Each angel can only be "stolen" three times and then it is "frozen." At the time of this annual gift exchange a side of the Spurs comes out we don't ever see the rest of the year! Some temporarily lose the meaning of grace! We laugh to the point of tears! In addition to wonderful and fond memories to cherish, we have a collection of many beautiful Yuletide angels that we have wrestled and fought for over the years!

Gayle O'Neal hoped she would get to keep this angel.

Sally Renshaw took it away from Gayle O'Neal as her choice.

Molly Dummit was the third and final owner
of Gayle and Sally's angel.

The heart of our Christmas gathering occurs as we gather around a beautiful crèche designed and made by a special wood worker in Fort Worth over thirty years ago. It has the Star of David carved on one end to remind us that Jesus was Jewish. Some friends made a little "Jesulein" or baby Jesus for us. He royally resides in the manger for most of December draped in purple.

We always sing "Away in the Manger," a cappella, as we gather around the manger. I love it too, when we sing a lesser-known song, but still one of my favorites. The words are:

> *"The empty come to Jesus, with love they go away:*
> *So they have love to offer, to all who come their way."*

After a holy prayer, we exchange hugs and warm Christmas blessings to seal our hearts for the busy days ahead. We "go away" full—full from a delicious meal but more importantly, full to overflowing for the blessing of gathering together with precious friends to remember, worship and celebrate the birth of Jesus and the salvation He brings.

A Time for THE Gift
A Gift to the Spurs
by Carolyn Boyd

Dawn of Redeeming Grace

For centuries the world sat in darkness
Trying to find the way.
The prophets who spoke were now silent—
They had said all there was to say.

Then God broke through the darkness and silence.
He found an obedient child.
To Mary the promise was given—
A babe will be born, meek and mild.

In awe she accepted this honor
Though the world viewed her with shame.
She bore God's son in a manger,
Over the world He would reign.

A light dawned into the world's great darkness.
Yet, how could it really know
What a difference the birth of a Savior
Would make to a world full of woe.

He grew full of wisdom and purpose
For He knew to a cross He would go.
He came as our example
That salvation from sin we could know.

His light shined in my personal darkness.
He showed me how to be free.
His light then guided my footsteps—
At last I was able to see!

How could the world possibly know
At that very first Christmastime
That the glorious Christ child was given—
God's love for all mankind to show.

It was the dawn of redeeming grace.
Its meaning I know just in part.
I've lived in the light of that new day
As I've taken Him into my heart.

When I measure my life by His righteousness,
I soon begin to see
The depths of Love's redeeming grace
Which covers my sin so completely.

So, let us rejoice and sing once again
The words from that old refrain,
"Radiant beams from Thy Holy face,
With the dawn of redeeming grace,
Christ the Savior is born.
Christ the Savior is born."

Spurred by Grace
Chapter Twelve

A Time for Heaven

A Time to Release to Eternal Love   by Maureen Eagan
A Time to Prepare   by Georgia Smith
A Time to Remember   by Carolyn Boyd
A Time for Precious Memories   by Kathleen Page Clark
A Time to Let Go and Let God   by Barbara Clarkin

A Time to Release to Eternal Love

by Maureen Eagan

Jesus said to her, "Your brother [husband, son and grandson]
will rise again."
John 11:23 (words in brackets added by Maureen)

I will not leave you comfortless.
John 14:18 (KJV)

*S*omewhere on my journey through losses, I heard, read or was told this phrase: "Death is part of life."

When my seven-year-old son, Rex, ran into my bedroom late at night, he had fears about death. He was afraid that I might die before he does. I gasped inwardly and prayed for a good answer for him—and God gave me this picture. "Rex, heaven and earth are like a two-story house. As long as we live here on earth, we are living on the first, ground floor. When one of us dies, they go through the door that leads to the upstairs and they go up. We can't see them anymore, but we know they are 'up there' and we are in the same 'house!' I will probably die first. When I do go up the 'stairs', I'll be waiting for you at the top!" Rex backed off, looked at me and said, "I bet I know what you will say!" "What?" I asked. "You'll say, where on earth have you been?" What started with tears and fears ended in laughter—and I have used that illustration many times since.

Little did I know that I would recall this childlike image of Heaven when dealing with the death of three family members: my husband, Woody, in 1992; my son, Rex, in 2008; and my grandson,

Zach in 2010. Where would I be without my God, a mature belief in Heaven, and the Spurs?

Here are my words of "Thanks" to and for the Spurs, taken from a letter I wrote at Easter after Woody, my beloved husband, died:

> *"Your love has literally surrounded us with God's promise: I will not leave you desolate or comfortless. This promise takes on new meaning for us this year as our aching hearts are fully assured. We can have true joy in our sorrow because we know our Lord Jesus Christ, Woody, and the rest of the Spurs' loved ones who have gone on before us have risen! Hallelujah!"*

Little did I know that I would later be saying these same words to these same dear Spurs when my son, Rex, and my grandson, Zach, died. Yes, they have gone on ahead—risen to a new life in Christ—where they wait for me in Heaven. I expect Rex to greet me at the top of the stairs with his childlike view of Heaven and say to me, "Where on earth have you been?"

Barbara Clarkin, a Spur, sent me a greeting card that said it so beautifully: As you remember the love, as you mourn the loss, may you also celebrate the life!

Then she added a personal note:

> *As Zach now rests in the Lord, the loved ones behind mourn their loss until it is realized how glorious he now is in his new body. You all had loving support and spiritual sup-port over these last painful weeks, but your prayers were answered for a peaceful death with loved ones there. We continue to be here for you.*
> *Love, Barbara and Walter*

Barbara can truly express these feelings as she, herself, buried her adult son after a long illness with ALS.

The Spurs continue to "be here for each other" and to "spur

one another on to do good works." We strengthen each other and help to pick up life with both hands and continue!

I continue to declare: "Hallelujah! They are risen—and so shall we be!"

A Time to Prepare

(Georgia's funeral arrangements)

by Georgia Smith

I can never escape from your Spirit!
I can never get away from your presence!
If I go up to heaven, you are there;
If I go down to the grave, you are there.
Psalm 139:7-8 (NLT)

Georgia wrote her funeral arrangements sixteen years before she died on November 27, 2010. We are including it here as her story for this book.

It is best to read it in her own handwriting!

Oh, that we will all be this prepared!

Nov. 2, 1994

Georgia Smith funeral request

Dearest Ted,

This is going to be one of the strangest letters you'll ever get. There is no other way to say it, than to say it. I've been thinking & planning ahead for my, don't faint, funeral service. Since I don't know when that will happen, I should have the pleasure of helping to plan for it. I want everything that is said or done to be used to Glorify My Lord! I may add to this along. I have probably already said too much. I never have learned yet how to be brief. I adore the 139 Psalm. If it is appropriate I would like to have that reader printed whatever you think. When I heard Bob Harless sing "Find Us Faithful," I certainly choose that song. Another favorite is "Take My Life". One of my very most favorites is "O, How He Loves You and Me". Everytime we sing it in Church it touches my heart and brings a tear. If Joey Harris is still around, he would be perfect for that one. Maybe you should just sing the whole service or better still

Georgia's letter to her pastor, Ted Kitchens,
about her memorial wishes (part 1).

265

have Lewis to compose a special
funeral Cantatta for me. Ha!!
That's all I can think of right now.
Oh you might add the harp, the
bell choir, the flute. Just kidding.
Just tell a bunch of good lies about
me. Opps sorry, you don't lie. Just
st-re-t-ch the truth a little.

I love you,
Georgia Struth

Georgia's letter to her pastor, Ted Kitchens,
about her memorial wishes (part 2).

A Time to Remember
Carolyn Driggers Mallone's Memorial Service
Written and delivered by Carolyn Boyd on September 18, 2007

*For I am the LORD, your God, who takes hold of your right hand
and says to you, Do not fear; I will help you.*
Isaiah 41:13 (NIV 1984)

*A*lthough Alzheimer's disease has claimed the life of our dear friend, Carolyn Driggers Mallone, our memories of her continue to bring joy to each of the Spurs. I was so blessed when David, her son, called and asked me to say some things about Carolyn. She was a *sparkling diamond* among us, always encouraging us or making us laugh. We will miss her, but....

I like to remember—how beautiful she was and how beautiful were her surroundings. Whether she was decorating her house or creating a tropical paradise in her backyard, the result was always amazing. Spending time in her garden was a bit of heaven in her part of Arlington, Texas. Everyone enjoyed her artistry on that small plot of land.

I like to remember—the many, many friends she had. One in particular, whom Carolyn called "her sister," was Sandra Talkington. Sandra was the one who introduced Carolyn to the Spurs. The Spurs are a group of women who chose the following scripture to be our collective life verse.

*And let us consider how we may **spur** one another on toward
love and good deeds. Let us not give up meeting together,
as some are in the habit of doing, but let us encourage one
another—and all the more as you see the Day approaching.*
Hebrews 10:24-25 (NIV 1984)

I like to remember—what Carolyn brought to the group. She
always brought joy and laughter. She taught me so much about
what *Grace* truly means. I can't remember ever hearing a judg-
mental word coming from her mouth as she loved and encouraged each of us as no one else could. She encouraged us with her
unconditional love, with prayer and with scripture. Scripture was
her guide for life. She often quoted Isaiah 41:13.

*For I am the LORD your God, who takes hold of your right
hand and says to you, 'Do not fear, I will help you.'*

Carolyn also loved Isaiah 40:31.

*Those who hope in the LORD will renew their strength.
They will soar on wings like eagles; they will run and not
grow weary, they will walk and not faint.*

She walked so closely with God and knew Him so well, that
when Carolyn spoke, we listened.

I like to remember—how she struggled about writing a book.
After Hugh, her first husband, died so many things happened in
which she saw the hand of God so she began writing about her
journey. In her quiet times she felt God calling her to write a book
but she argued with the Lord, saying, "I can't write a book – I'm
a terrible speller." She continued to pray about it and the Lord
convinced her she should do this. One day I received a phone
call—it was Carolyn. She asked if I could help her put her story
on paper. So, with my computer and "spell-check" on hand, we
traveled to Colorado to write her book. We spent a glorious week
in Colorado writing and rewriting those chapters and during the

whole time having a mountaintop experience with the Lord as we plunged ahead with this project. That book eventually became half the book entitled *Hearts on Pilgrimage*, which tells her story. Later she met and married George Mallone and he wrote his side of the story showing God's hand in their lives.

I like to remember—taking wonderful trips with the Spurs. Colorado was a favorite destination of the Spurs, but whether it was taking a day trip to Tyler, Texas, to see the azaleas or traveling to England to walk through the Cotswolds, Carolyn brought joy and laughter to every shared experience. I especially remember on the trip to walk in the Cotswolds, we started out one day with rain slickers and umbrellas. We began our traipse through what we called "Sherwood Forest." We were told it was just a short walk through the woods to an English Pub where we could find lunch—so off we went. Two hours later we emerged from the forest to see the little village for which we had been searching. Drenched to the bone from the downpour, we went into the Pub where we encountered an all-male bicycling club having their lunch. The attractive redhead immediately got their attention. We joked that Carolyn just might find a husband among them.

Another day on that same trip, the Spurs split into two groups—one group was going to Stratford-upon-Avon while the other was going to the quaint town of Broadway. Those of us who had been to Stratford told the other group what the "*must sees*" were, and even gave them a list. That evening, upon their return, we asked how they had enjoyed Anne Hathaway's Cottage, Shakespeare's home, etc. only to find they hadn't seen anything we had suggested! Instead, they had had tea and conversation at an outdoors "tea room" just enjoying the English people. That was Carolyn—always more interested in people than historic sites.

I like to remember—when it was decided Carolyn needed to move somewhere where her environment would be more pro-tective and we felt she needed something to love. Three Spurs, Sandra, Molly and I, bought the Betty Miliken doll that was adver-tised as *someone to love*. When we took it to her, we told her we had named the doll "Joy" because she had brought so much joy to each of us. Even though she had not been able to talk for months, she clearly said, "No! Grace!" Grace, it would be. Indeed, grace was the hallmark of Carolyn's life.

Finally, *I like to remember*—when some of us went to see her in her new abode in Hurst, Texas. We told her how much we loved her and reminisced about our good times together. We then began singing hymns to her. When we started singing, although she was no longer communicating, she held Molly's hand and kept a perfect beat with our singing. Her spirit was in agreement with the praise of the songs and she was responding the only way she could.

Well, the struggle was long for Carolyn and her family, but the picture I have of her today is one of happiness and joy as she is embraced by all those she loved who had gone before her and it is the place of pure joy and love. She is in the presence of Jesus and is whole.

I like to remember you, Carolyn.

Left to right: Carolyn Driggers Mallone and Carolyn Boyd.

A Time for Precious Memories

by Kathleen Page Clark

Precious in the sight of the LORD is the death of his saints.
Psalm 116:15

The Spurs are an aging group of ladies. While we have raised our children, grandchildren and great-grandchildren together with prayer, it has become a season of ushering more and more Spurs into Heaven. We celebrate their homecoming but we also comfort each other in our loss. Each Spur is a sister and so each departed one leaves a significant hole in our future gatherings.

We were all in great hopes that this book would be published before another Spur's name was added to the memorial page. It did not happen but we are pleased that Mary Jo knew it was to be a reality before her passing.

As with all occasions, the Spurs show up. The Spurs and their husbands were a significant section of people that filled Mary Jo's church for her celebration of life. We continue to celebrate her life eternal with her Lord and Savior Jesus Christ.

Below, is a tribute her children wrote for her service:

Mary Jo Scheideman, 81, had no greater priority than a life-long, heartfelt and purposeful commitment to Jesus Christ our Lord and Savior.

Mary Jo Israel was born April 13, 1931, in Wichita, Kan., to Jay and Margaret Israel. She attended Kansas University, and while there she pledged Kappa Kappa Gamma, majored in social work, and met Blaine Scheideman, fresh from the wheat fields of western Kansas. They married on Dec. 20, 1952, and were newlyweds in Kansas before moving to Fort Wayne, Ind., and eventually Fort Worth. Fort Worth was always home, but Blaine's career at General Dynamics took them many places from Dayton, Ohio, to Brussels, Belgium, before returning to Fort Worth to retire.

While in California, her good friend June Fawell introduced her to Mother Basilea of the Evangelical Sisterhood of Mary, and her life changed as she understood and embraced the gospel. She shared the Sisters' passion for the gospel as well as their scripture bookmarks with everyone she knew or met, distributing these encouraging words indiscriminately to a dear friend, a casual acquaintance, or the nighttime attendant at the rehabilitation facility. Wherever she went, Mary Jo shared the love of Jesus. She started Bible studies and prayer groups in whatever town she called home.

As Blaine's work required them to travel, Mary Jo quickly adapted and embraced new people, cultures, cities and adventures. An only child, she always wanted a large family. With three children, nine grandchildren, and two great-grandchildren, she had that and so much more. Mary Jo loved and prayed for her family, and they loved spending time with "Nanny." By God's provision, and through Mary Jo's organization and planning skills, they took the whole family on many trips. Her spunkiness and sense of adventure has been passed on to them and will be to the generations to come.

Mary Jo lived a life of faith, praying fervently for those around her. She was a member at St. Paul Lutheran Church, Ft. Worth, Texas, for over 45 years. Her greatest joy was her family and friends, and she jumped at every opportunity to use her home to bless others.

She passed from this life to the next surrounded by the family for which she had always hoped.

Mary Jo Scheideman

A Time to Let Go and Let God

by Barbara Clarkin

.....My peace I give you......
Do not let your hearts be troubled and do not be afraid.
John 14:27

"*L*et go, let God" was a favorite quote of a friend of mine. I never dreamed that fourteen years after my second marriage, I would have learned to do just that.

This is a story of a journey of two people embracing that quote. It began on May 26, 1996, the date that celebrates our marriage and a new beginning for two older people. Walter and I looked forward to being together for however long the Lord gave us. We were so happy to have all of our families (which included my thirty-one grandchildren and his two grandchildren) and many of our friends witness our marriage. We had decided to delay our honeymoon in order to celebrate on the Monday after Memorial Day with our families at a backyard picnic. It was rare for my sister, brother, their spouses and my children and their children to be able to visit Texas at the same time. It was a joyful reunion and the future looked so bright.

There were many conversations that Monday, but one in particular between my sons Kevin and David, an internist, caught my attention. Kevin was a computer systems analyst and had been experiencing numbness and tingling in his arms which he attributed to possible Carpal Tunnel Syndrome, a condition common to his type of work. After relating this to David, he asked if it was possible to have these symptoms also involve the shoulder areas. David asked him if he had any other unusual physical problems. The answer was that he sometimes slurs his words. David then asked to see him in his office at 8 a.m. the next day.

The next morning, Kevin arrived and after a short examination David sent him to a neurologist with whom David had already made an appointment. This would be the first of many tests over the next couple of weeks.

While Kevin began his tests, Walter and I left on a weeklong cruise with two of our grandchildren. This was an event that started in 1987 with the first two grandchildren when they were ages nine and eleven. These cruises are a real bonding experience for us. Walter and I have taken nineteen cruises with thirty-seven grandchildren. It is 2011 and we have only one more cruise to go, but by the time this four-year-old granddaughter is old enough, she may have to push both of our wheelchairs!

On the day after we left, Kevin also started serving a six-month jail sentence for allegedly trespassing at a local Planned Parenthood facility. He had been involved for a year and a half with Operation Rescue, a group of peaceful demonstrators representing the unborn. He spent quite a few weekend days in jail with some of the other members. A judge sentenced six of them to jail following the last demonstration. They were allowed to work but had to spend nights and weekends in a cell. Kevin's mantra was a verse from Acts 5:29 (KJV), "We ought to obey God rather than men." He was a solid warrior for our Lord.

After we returned from our trip, I was becoming alarmed by some of the test results Kevin was receiving. I was a nurse and it didn't sound good to me, but I put my trust in God that everything would be OK. Easier said than done! Finally two weeks later the diagnosis was returned, "Amyotrophic Lateral Sclerosis," commonly known as "Lou Gehrig's Disease." We were devastated as we knew the cause was unknown, that there was not a cure and that the life span was anywhere from one to ten years depending on the area of the body that was first afflicted. Kevin's life span was estimated at five to seven years. Where oh where was God when I needed him most? As I am a very organized and practical person I immediately started planning for all eventualities. Of course, I prayed but I did not turn my anxieties over to the Lord.

The founder of Operation Rescue communicated with the judge who sentenced Kevin to jail. Then the judge decided to terminate the jail stay and put Kevin on house arrest whereby he still worked days but spent nights and weekends with an ankle locator at home. Kevin declined this offer as he had started a ministry with other cellmates but that was denied. Kevin wrote a letter to all of his co-workers explaining his condition and asked them not to treat him any differently as his physical abilities diminished. He ended by stating, "I am not dead yet." That put all of them at ease and kept them in the loop on both his prognosis and awareness of the disease in general. Kevin now adopted a new mantra, a verse from Joshua 1:9, which is: "Be strong and of a good courage; be not afraid." (KJV) I found myself trying to assimilate that verse for myself.

Walter and I visited the Holy Land the following year. We visited Lake Tiberius where I gathered stones from the shore and brought them back to give to my Spur family to hold in their hands daily and pray for a miracle. They were so faithful with their prayers and their concern for all of us. I also had all of my church congregation praying and many others who eventually heard about the situation. There were prayers all over the country. What faithful friends I had, as did Kevin! Kevin's friends and church members were also very supportive. My prayer life continued to increase.

I worried about his three children, ages one, three and five, and his wife. How will they survive the effects of this disease on their lives? They would need so much support over the next few years. My former husband, a cardiologist, was wealthy and generous so I knew that finances would not be a total burden. Kevin sold his home in Arlington and bought one in Fort Worth closer to his family so there would be help in the days ahead. He continued to work and was quite ingenious in adapting to his continuing disabilities. We all helped as best we could. I even changed a hard drive in a computer with his guidance while he was doing outside consulting work striving to earn more money to leave his family.

He also continued to take the family on camping trips and adventures. One day he realized that there would be less interaction with the children. There would be times when he could no longer throw a basketball into the net when playing with his son. His speech was so compromised that communication was difficult.

Kevin was subsequently accepted into a research program in Houston. This meant that there would be monthly and then weekly trips to the clinic. Two years later he was chosen as one of seven men in a trial in which they were to receive bone marrow transplants from a sibling with an exact match. Kevin was one of three out of the seven with exact matches. Out of his five siblings, only one, his fraternal twin sister, Kerin, matched even though they were not of the same blood type. She had just had a miscarriage and was quite depressed but when she found out she was his only hope in the experiment she realized that God's hand was definitely in control for if she had been pregnant she would not have been accepted. Eventually Kevin was the only survivor in this trial group. When three more patients were chosen for the same test, only one of them survived. Since there were just two that lived, the research was cancelled.

Following the transplant Kevin spent four months at his brother Steve's home in Houston in semi-isolation. During this time he contracted pneumonia three times, losing two-thirds of his lung capacity and a tremendous amount of weight. He eventually had to have a feeding tube inserted and became dependent on a breathing machine during the night. It appeared that the bone marrow transplant had worsened his condition. I know Kevin still trusted the Lord with the outcome, but I was losing faith in a miracle as a possibility.

After Kevin returned home, his mood swings started and his anger was often out of control. He was frustrated at his inability to control his body and was not trusting God. I was ashamed at the way he was treating his caregivers but realized that I was not in control of that situation and turned it over to God. His twin sister and I would arrange trips to Virginia to her home for R&R for both he and his wife. During one of these trips, his wife moved out of the house taking the children with her and did not announce her intentions or her destination. We were all angry and perplexed. A divorce followed and the house sold when it was apparent we were not going to be able to find twenty-four hour a day caregivers.

Kevin agreed to come and live with Walter and me. Walter was like a father and a compassionate caregiver for him. Everything was working out well. We were able to create an office area in his room so that he might continue his computer activities, which was the only activity he could perform. Kevin continued to be in control of all his business matters though I had become his Power of Attorney, as he could not write checks, etc. His progress deteriorated over the next ten months to the point where he was on oxygen frequently and eventually on the breathing apparatus twenty-two hours a day. I then hired part-time help as we rarely had more than two to three hours of sleep at a time. I also was not quite physically strong enough as he required more physical help in all he did. Although he had decided almost from the beginning of his disease that he would not want extra measures to keep him alive, he now changed his mind because of his children who needed strong parenting and he was the one trying to do that. He went to Dallas for a procedure that involved a tracheotomy and a ventilator being installed to aid him in his breathing. No longer would he have to rely on oxygen tanks and breathing machines. A couple of his part-time caregivers, several siblings and Walter and I were trained to operate the equipment. Kevin required procedures every four hours initially, then decreased to three to four times a week.

After several weeks at home, Kevin decided it was too much for us. He also wanted to feel more independent so asked to go to a care facility. The family saw the possibility of damage to a parent-child relationship so insisted that I honor his request. There was only one nursing home in the area that could care for vent patients. We admitted him only to find out they had antiquated equipment and would not allow our equipment to be used. Ten days later he had pneumonia and a staph infection and was in ICU, so we removed him from their service. Then began what would be a search for one of four private care facilities that he would live in over the next four years. We located one that was not licensed, as the state would not allow licensed homes to take vent patients. Nursing homes would not take them either unless you provided a private care person to be with him twenty-four hours a day. That was unaffordable. If I had had the energy and the time I would have started a process that would hope-fully change the way in which patients with ventilators would have licensed facilities available to them. At this time I was also becoming agitated with the way Kevin would sometimes treat his caregivers. I needed to trust more that God was in control!

The final home Kevin was to occupy was one that my former husband and I agreed to rent and have one of his faithful care-givers move in and start a home care business for herself. We found a location in Fort Worth, closer to our family in order to have more help. The other three homes had been closer to his children but as they grew older and were still dependent on transportation for visits, they came less often. Kevin was unhappy with this latest arrangement. His disease had so progressed that I could no longer take him to athletic events or activities of his chil-dren. He also began missing the family holiday gatherings. I was visiting as often as possible but not so much that he refused some of the care from the caregivers. Walter and I were still his hands and feet in many ways. A year later his condition progressed to the point that he could only operate a special computer with his eyelids. He had a healthy mind trapped in a useless body.

It had been over thirteen and a half years by now and he was exhausted by all of it and to some extent we were also. I began to pray for a peaceful demise. Thanksgiving of that year Kevin told me he was ready to have the ventilator removed. The previous year I had selected two plots at a cemetery for both of us and he had written his funeral arrangements. He was ready for death and expressed his sorrow that his children no longer looked to him as their father. I asked him to address all of the family at Christmas about this matter. He did and conversations that fol-lowed convinced five of his siblings enough that they agreed with him. The eldest, an Episcopal priest, his father and I were not so sure. His father was upset stating that he had been saving lives for over fifty years and was not going to be a part of ending one. His brother thought that Kevin still demonstrated productivity in his life with his intelligent decisions and writings. I thought that as a Catholic, the faith of which is against suicide, that Kevin's decision might be misinterpreted as one. We eventually agreed that we would support him in his choice. He set a date of March 17, 2009.

I was certainly apprehensive about my feelings that I would be a part of an assisted suicide. I made an appointment with my pastor. After telling him the story he said that Kevin had made the decision to continue to sustain life with artificial means and he had the right to discontinue those means. If God's plan was to take Kevin's life earlier He could have. If God's plan was for Kevin to die after removal of the life support, Kevin would possibly, although against odds, continue to live by breathing on his own. That day I felt a peace that I had not felt in some time. If Kevin had the courage to make this decision then why should I be afraid of the results? My troubled heart began to release its grip on me. It really was in God's hands.

Almost fourteen years after the diagnosis, the day had arrived to remove the equipment. All of the siblings and spouses had made their arrangements to be with him as well as many of the nieces and nephews. He had three months to facilitate business, write letters to friends and update his will. His children saw him more often and a peace in him that we had not witnessed in some time was becoming apparent. There was reconciliation to all those that he offended with his actions over the last several years, including his ex-wife. He wrote a manifesto of his life to be read and distributed at his memorial service. During the last week he made appointments on the hour to visit one-on-one with family and close friends. He had purchased a car for his eldest child as she was going on to college. He did it all online as he had been doing for many years. He was coordinating the last hours of what he perceived would be his last days on this earth and he was doing it with clarity.

On that day there was a feeling of heaviness in my heart as I thought of all the things I did not do that I might have done to help

Kevin. I had so enjoyed our times together driving to Houston and other doctors' appointments, watching movies, having conversations about sports, politics, our nation, our families and telling anecdotes from the past. I tried to focus on the new life and body he would now enjoy and almost envied the fact that he would be with the Lord and I would still be here. I still thought that parents should precede their children in death. We had arranged that Kevin would come home where he had grown up rather than stay in the care home for this final procedure. Family, friends, hospice personnel and ministers were all gathered. Kevin was being transported by van with his caregivers to the house and he was late! We all laughingly said, as we said many times before, that he would be late for his own funeral! (Tardiness had always been a habit of his).

Finally they arrived and the conversations commenced by way of the use of the alphabet board. There were hymns sung, scriptures read, stories told and then he signaled it was time to start the process after making one last request. He had not been able to hug his children for over three years and wanted to do so. They climbed upon his bed and I held his right arm around one of the girls and someone else held his other arm around another girl, while his son edged onto a space where he could hold his Dad around his waist. Kevin, with tears in his eyes, but a smile on his face blinked at David, his physician, to begin. A mild sedative was given to ease anxiety that might arise as his vent pressure was reduced and his breathing would become compromised. I held his head between my hands. I brought him into this world and now I would hold him until he left it, if that was to be. His heart continued to beat six minutes after the machine was off then the Lord took him home. It was a very peaceful death for him and for all there.

I thank God for all the blessings that had come from this experience and surprisingly there were more than a few. I thank God for my Spur family who were supportive for years. I thank God also for many other friends who were prayer warriors. I felt peace, no longer fearing what life would be without such a devoted son and no longer fearing what would happen next to him. Kevin had let go and let God and I knew that I had done the same. Until we meet again, every day I look at his engaging smile in the framed photograph that sits on my desk and I know his spirit is with me.

Left to right: Kevin Capper with mother Barbara Clarkin.

Spurred by Grace
Chapter Thirteen

A Time to Honor

A Time for Grace—Carolyn Driggers Mallone   by Sandra Talkington
A Time for Inspiration—Jeff Davis   by Mary Alice Brumley
A Time to Give Tribute—Suzie Martin Murray   by Mary Alice Brumley
A Time for a Perfect Friend—Georgia Smith   by Pat Reynolds

A Time for Grace
In loving memory of Carolyn Driggers Mallone
by Sandra Talkington

Have I not commanded you? "Be strong and courageous!
Do not tremble or be dismayed, for the Lord your God
is with you wherever you go."
Joshua 1:9 (NASB)

One of our Spurs is not here to write her story, so I will try to give you a picture of Carolyn Driggers Mallone and her faith. Carolyn was a beautiful redhead who was artistic, creative and lots of fun. She loved her garden and created a gorgeous fountain out of the pool she no longer wanted. It was surrounded by a brick courtyard that was flanked by azaleas, crepe myrtles, rich foliage, and lots of blooming plants—a beautiful place to sit and talk in her swing or on the patio. We spent many hours talking and praying for our families and friends.

Her home was just as beautiful and inviting, decorated in her unique style and with some of her original paintings and handiwork. The same was true of her style of dress, for which she had a real flair.

That is probably one reason she was asked to do a Bible study for the girls at Bauder Fashion College. This enabled the girls to relate and be drawn to her. Her main qualification was her love for the Lord. Her study was very successful.

Carolyn became a Christian as an adult and was such an enthusiastic and bold witness for Christ. She went through the five year Bible Study Fellowship program, was very active in her Sunday school class and in her Bible Church, was in a prayer group that was very dear to her, and became a Spur, which she called, "family."

As a Spur, we do feel like sisters. We have been together for over thirty-five years and have bonded through both laughter and tears.

Carolyn was a dear friend to me and a neighbor as well. Our children went to school together. We sat on benches at games together. We both had a love of gardening and shared plants and ideas with each other. I still have some of her daylilies growing in my garden.

We became spiritual friends, also. We were in the same group in Bible Study Fellowship our first year. That is when our friendship started to grow. In our Spurs group, Carolyn often had just the right Scripture to add light to a situation.

It was very difficult to accept when I was told that Carolyn was diagnosed with Alzheimer's dementia in her mid-fifties. At first, I didn't believe it. As time passed, however, it became obvious that it was true.

In 1998, the Spurs, our Christian share group, were planning a trip to Italy. Although Carolyn had been diagnosed with Alzheimer's dementia, she was still able to enjoy being with close friends. Because of her fear of becoming disoriented and possibly separated from the group, she was very hesitant to go. I assured her that we would not let that happen. Finally, she agreed to go with us. It was a wonderful trip and would be the last trip like that she would be able to take. We were roommates and had a wonderful view of the Tuscan countryside from our balcony in the villa where we were staying.

There was one moment in which my heart sank. Four of us in the group who worked for an airline had gone on ahead. Carolyn was traveling with four others in the group. They had promised to not let Carolyn out of their sight. We were to meet up on the train from Milan to Venice. When I first laid eyes on the other group, I quickly discerned that there were only three and Carolyn wasn't one of them. My heart sank! They apologized over and over and quickly assured me that Carolyn and Phyllis, in the confusion of the foreign train station, had taken another train to Venice.

When we came down the steps of the train station, there were Carolyn and Phyllis. What a joy and sense of relief! The rest of the trip was wonderful, visiting Venice, Florence, and many of the quaint little towns of Tuscany. Carolyn thoroughly enjoyed strolling through the narrow streets, stopping for a gelato, listening to a harpist in the plaza, and going through churches that had existed since the Middle Ages.

As the years went by, Carolyn's disease progressed. She had much difficulty with her speech. In fact, we had been together so much, I usually knew what she was trying to say and would try to help her. There were two instances in which Carolyn didn't need any help at all. Once, when we were meeting in the home of a Spur, she prayed the most beautiful and fervent prayer for the son of a Spur. On another occasion, she prayed for the grandchild of another Spur without even a stammer. It was apparent that the Holy Spirit was her Helper. Needless to say, it was very inspiring to all of us.

Several of us would sing hymns to her from time to time when we went to see her. The last time we sang to her, she couldn't sing, but she held Molly's hand and kept time with the music. It warmed our hearts to see her response.

Carolyn passed from this life in August 2008. We miss her physical presence with us more than we could ever express, but will never forget the many wonderful times we have shared together. We look forward to a joyous reunion with her in Heaven someday!

Left to right: Sandra Talkington and Carolyn Driggers Mallone.

A Time for Inspiration
In loving memory of Jeff Davis, son of Spur Molly Dummit
by Mary Alice Brumley

And He said to them,
"Go into all the world and preach the gospel to all creation."
Mark 16:15 (NASB)

*I*n the early 1990s, I had the opportunity to go with Jeff Davis, Molly's son, and a team of volunteers, doctors and dentists on a Medical Mission Trip to Mexico. Our destination was the Copper Canyon. We left early one morning from Garland and Molly Dummit's house, loaded with every kind of medical supply and gear that you can imagine. Those of you who know Molly know that we left Fort Worth with all of our needs met. Their son, Jeff, was driving the lead van and the rest of the team followed in the second van with Garland, Molly's husband, at the wheel. Our first challenge was to get across the border without having our supplies confiscated. We made it across safely and shot up a quick prayer as we drove down the road into Mexico. That was the first miracle.

The Copper Canyon was our destination. It is at least three times larger than the Grand Canyon and it is rugged, massive and breathtaking in its remarkable beauty. When the sun hits the walls of the canyon, it reflects a beautiful copper color, thus giving it the name. The next challenge that we faced was to get to the bottom of the canyon so we could minister to the Taramahara Indians who live there. Our two small airplanes were loaded to capacity with generators, cooking supplies, water, food, medical supplies and movie projectors to show the Jesus film. We even had a dental chair. There is no running water or electricity in the canyon. We were to sleep in tents on the floor of the canyon and we were to be there working together for almost a week.

Our team had commissioned two pilots to fly us into the canyon. One of our pilots was a missionary supported by our church who lives close to the canyon. He and his children were our translators. The other was a very young Canadian pilot. The pilots had to spiral downward into the bottom of the canyon to land the planes on a runway that had been cut out on the top of a mesa by drug lords. Garland was in the co-pilot's seat and I was in the only seat in the back of the plane. As our plane descended into the canyon, we were coming in too fast to stop before we ran out of runway. There were mountains in front of us and a deep gorge at the end of the runway, so either way, we were in trouble. Because of my position in the plane, I couldn't see any of this but all of a sudden I heard Garland yelling, "I'll see you in a minute, Jesus! I'll see you in a minute, Jesus!" Jamie, the pilot, knew we were in trouble. Somehow, he stopped the plane just short of going over the edge of the cliff. The Indian children from the village ran after our plane and were cheering and clapping as we sat inside praising God that we were still alive. That was the second miracle.

The very next day in the village, Jeff and I set up the medical supplies in a one-room shack. We assisted Dr. Garland Dummit who saw over seventy patients that first day. I never saw Jeff sit down or take a break but he insisted that I take one. He and Garland worked so well together. They had a mutual respect for each other and worked as a team. Jeff greeted each patient with kindness and with a smile. He was soft spoken and a very gentle but a strong man. Even though he did not speak the same language, he communicated his caring and compassion while doing whatever had to be done.

Garland died the next year after the mission trip. His minute was up. God says in His word, that He has numbered all of our days. I know He had just the right number of days and minutes for Jeff as well. After Jeff died, Molly and I were reflecting on why now, at Christmas, Lord? Well, this is the season of gift giving. Jesus is a gift to anyone who will believe and receive Him. The wise men brought gifts to Jesus. They were really the first gift givers to celebrate Jesus' birth.

What a great way to remember Jeff as we receive our gifts from each other at Christmas. Jeff was the bearer of gifts to the Taramahara Indians where I got to serve with him and watch his joy in ministering with his gifts to others. Our mission team presented the gift of salvation to the Indians of the Copper Canyon. Molly and Elizabeth (Molly's daughter and Jeff's sister) have given me the gift of friendship and I joined them in their prayers for Jeff for almost thirty years. Jeff, Molly's son, was a gift from the Lord just as Zach, Jeff's son, was a gift to him. Jeff is sharing eternity with Jesus because he accepted the gift of salvation and the Lord has taken him safely home. Jeff was my friend and he inspired me with his gift of service and love for others until his minute was up.

Left to right: Brother Jeff Davis and sister Elizabeth Buckley.

Left to right: Jeff Davis and Pat Reynolds.

A Time to Give Tribute
In memory of my fun and loving friend, Spur Suzie Martin Murray
by Mary Alice Brumley

.......Bless the LORD, O my soul, and all that is within me,
bless his holy name.
Psalm 103:1 (NASB)

"*If* you knew Suzie, like I know Suzie, Oh, Oh, Oh, what a gal! There's none as classy as this fair lassie, Oh, Oh, Oh, what a gal!" I have always thought those words described Suzie perfectly. She was the very essence of a "Southern Belle" and even though she had lived in Texas for over thirty years, she never lost her southern Alabama accent or her undeniable southern charm. Suzie was as glamorous as a movie star with her natural beauty. She was a gracious, kind, loving and genteel friend. I miss her terribly! Suzie went to be with our Lord, December 31, 2009.

Suzie loved her family and her friends and she loved life. Life is about living, and she lived it to the fullest. She loved to dance and she also loved to sing. I remember on one of our Spur trips together, we were singing all the old songs that we knew. It was Suzie who knew the lyrics and tunes to every one of them. She never missed a word or a note. I told her what a great gift I thought it was and what a great mind she had to remember all those songs. She quickly quipped that she was only good at the mundane things of life.

What really defines our lives and reveals our character are the challenges we face and how we then live. Suzie's life was not without challenges. The last years of her life she suffered with tremendous physical pain. She always managed to have a smile on her face and a twinkle in her eye in spite of her pain. She was the kind of person you were always glad to see and that you would gladly meet under any circumstance.

Psalm 103 was Suzie's favorite bible passage. It portrays a lot about her character and her eternal perspective. Through all her pain and trials, she never lost her faith. She memorized this psalm and would say it over and over while she was taking her chemotherapy treatments. The first five verses read, "Bless the Lord, O my soul and all that is within me. Bless His Holy Name. Bless the Lord, O my soul and forget none of His benefits: Who pardons all your iniquities; Who heals all your diseases; Who redeems your life from the pit; Who crowns you with loving kindness and compassion; Who satisfies your years with good things, so that your youth is renewed like the eagle. Bless the Lord, O my soul."

Suzie began her final journey on this earth on the wings of an eagle in the form of a Coast Guard helicopter as she was airlifted off a cruise ship to a hospital in Miami. At the dawn of New Year's Eve morn, she was escorted into Heaven to begin the biggest celebration of her life—spending eternity with Jesus Christ. I will always count it as one of the greatest privileges and joys of my life to have known and loved Suzie. We are best friends.

"There's none as classy as this fair lassie, Oh, Oh, Oh what a gal!"

Suzanne (Suzie) Martin Murray

A Time for a Perfect Friend

In loving memory of Georgia Smith becoming a Spur

by Pat Reynolds

Most important of all, continue to show deep love for each other,
for love covers a multitude of sins.
Cheerfully share your home with those who need
a meal or a place to stay.
God has given each of you a gift from his great variety
of spiritual gifts.
Use them well to serve one another.
1 Peter 4:8-10

I remember when Georgia became a Spur. Ann Hyde approached me about wanting Georgia to be a part of our group. At the time we had some unfinished business that I believed needed closure before inviting a new person. It was not that Georgia couldn't be a Spur; it was more about timing. Then Carolyn Boyd contacted me, wanting to know "why" I thought Georgia Smith should not join us.

I didn't really have the authority to decide who became a Spur and who didn't. It has been somewhat of a mystery how our group came to be. We don't have a policy on adding Spurs. In fact, Phyllis White showed up in Italy as a new Spur. I like the way the Spurs "hang loose" about expanding the group. We have become closed, I think, by being fully occupied with the fairly large group we already have. Creating a larger group has never been a goal in itself. We don't have written rules, and our decisions are fluid, flowing in different directions. In Georgia's case, there was a strong tide of desire in our group to have her be a part of us, so she did. When Georgia joined us, she was the oldest Spur.

The first meeting she attended, she sat across the table from me at Sandra Talkington's house. She was so open and guileless, and I quickly knew why she was so special to those who knew her. She brought the number of TCU "infiltrators" to four—Gayle, Sally, Phyllis and Georgia. She also filled out our West Texas quintet, to Sally, Sandra, Pat, Janet, and now Georgia.

I loved going to visit Georgia and Billy Joe Smith. The Spurs met at the Smith's about once or twice a year. I remember a retreat where twelve of us slept in the big room over the garage. We all had a bed to sleep in, but only one bathroom! However that trip was never enough for me, and I have had many side trips to the Smith's ranch near Brock, Texas. The hospitality and pleasantness of Georgia and Billy Joe—and of course Sugie, Billy Joe's dog—gave a frequent rise in my heart calling me to run away to Brock.

Their ten-year-old French farmhouse that sat on a bluff overlooking seven hundred acres could bring peace and tranquility to any troubled soul. If you were a joyful soul, that joy would be increased. As you looked at the contented longhorns grazing in the pasture, you knew that if humans used these longhorns for milk consumption, it would be the best in the land!

I did need to learn a few admission tricks to keep my ticket useable. When I called, I never asked for Billy Smith. The Caller ID would show "unknown" and they would not talk to me. I must say both names: Billy Joe. After I got that trick down, I learned another one. I would call up and say: "Sugie (the dog) has been missing me and she wanted to know when I was going to come see her." That amused them and the invitation was always extended!

To get hold of Georgia and Billy Joe, I needed to call them before six in the morning. Every morning, they would be off to the local country café, meeting new and old friends. There were times that this provided them with workers for building their house. Once while Georgia was sick, I could reach them easily.

I did think my admission tricks were working, as I was never turned down. The real truth is that Billy Joe and Georgia are wonderful, hospitable people who love people. My mother used to talk about "real Texans." I know Georgia was born in Cassville, Missouri, but she and Billy Joe together smacked of being "real Texans." What you see is what you get. Being with Georgia and Billy Joe was like living in Fort Worth in the fifties—a more innocent, safer life, with a more neighborly flavor of caring.

Both Georgia and Billy Joe liked doing land development and building projects. I don't know much about building, but my understanding of building one room at a time is very different and something I had not heard of before. Georgia was a visual person. She needed to see the room built to determine how or if she needed to change it! So a room could be changed several times before it passed inspection. She asked me to pray for her, as she might be too demanding and perfectionistic.

Georgia was somewhat upset about the porch being in angles because she did not like angles. The Spurs, along with everybody else, thought the house was fabulous. It was decorated with Texas and Civil War memorabilia, antiques, unusual dishes, silver—an A to Z house! Georgia was an interior designer by nature and had a particular flair for putting things together. Her décor covered the waterfront. It was elegant, frontier and French country; she had an eye for scale, color and surprise!

On one of my leisure days, I thought I would call Georgia and pretend I was from *Southern Living* magazine. I said: "Hello. Is this Mrs. Billy Joe Smith of Brock, Texas?" "Yes," she replied. I then said: "Your house has been recommended as a possible feature in our magazine to demonstrate country living in Texas. Could you describe what style of house you have? Is it traditional or French Country?" I paused. Georgia replied with a little defensive upbeat in her voice. "Oh, you need to understand. I'm a Texan and I don't have one style of house. My house represents many styles." I then told her who I was and we both laughed!

Georgia did love beautiful things and her home would qualify for *Southern Living* magazine, but beautiful things were not her life. Jesus and people were her life—all kinds of people. She loved her four sons, their wives and her grandchildren, and her great-grandchildren. She also loved the Spurs.

Georgia had a simplicity about her that was pure. She had a graciousness and smile that would fill the room. You left her presence blessed and refreshed.

She put her hand in the hand of Jesus on November 27, 2010. On November 30, in the small town of Brock, Texas, we sat in a tin shed in a country cemetery, saying "Goodbye for now" to our precious Georgia.

The LORD cares deeply when his loved ones die.
Psalm 116:15 (NLT)

When Carolyn Boyd and Molly Dummit visited Georgia only weeks before her death, they asked her what words she would use to describe the Spurs. She said, "Perfect friends." I think Georgia was one of those perfect friends.

The love of God that she gave to all of us will last forever.

Left to right: Georgia Smith and Pat Reynolds.

Spurred by Grace
Chapter Fourteen

Children and Grandchildren of Spurs

A Time to Describe   by Jennifer Miller

A Time for a New Dream   by Karan Boyd Jamison

A Time to Thank the Spurs   by Kristin Page-Elliott Kirkland

A Time to Dance   by Debbie Boyd Petty

A Time for Answered Prayer   by Lisa O'Neal Hughes

A Time to Pass It On   by Karan Boyd Jamison

A Time to be Rodeo Queens   by Annie Laurie Hyde

A Time to Observe   by Hannah Jones

A Time of National Tragedy   by Keith Boyd

A Time to Describe

by Jennifer Miller

(daughter of Clarice Townes Miller)

But I am like an olive tree flourishing in the house of God;
I trust in God's unfailing love for ever and ever.
Psalm 52:8

am a daughter of a Spur. According to my brothers that makes me a "Spurette."

I have childhood memories of ladies' luncheons that Momma would host every so often. I didn't understand why they were getting together. I just knew we would have good chicken salad and rolls for afternoon snacks! The name "Spurs" intrigued me, but I was unaware of the community of heart that was growing.

I became more aware of the relationships of the Spurs when I went to college at Baylor and lived down the hall from another "Spurette." We became friends and I realized the friendships of these women were more than a ladies' luncheon group.

Time went on and I loved knowing Momma was part of these women who took their faith seriously, took their friendships seriously, and stuck it out with and for each other.

Over the years, I've been blessed to spend time with the Spurs. I went on a Mother-Daughter trip to Tuscany, Italy (funny thing—I was the only daughter). I've helped host them at Momma's home in Nacogdoches, hosted them at Camp DeSoto for a celebratory weekend (see the story titled "A Time to Rejoice"). I've been to several other Mother-Daughter events with other Spur daughters, too.

From spending time with the Spurs, this is what I know: There is no describing the Spurs in words. They are like the color black—they are the presence of ALL colors. Individually they are pretty incredible ladies who love their families, give to their communities, serve in their churches and encourage whoever is in their space. Collectively they are all these things but operating as a small picture of God's kingdom. They understand that true friendship requires sacrifice, suffering, laughter, tears, listening, being still, praying, sharing burdens, encouragement, being less, being more, and more laughter and more tears. They understand the whole is more important than any individual gain and that they desire to become more holy.

I chose Psalm 52:8 to describe the Spurs because they know to whom they belong. They know they are loved with God's unfailing love so they are free to love broadly. They share life's joys and sorrows. They remind each other of God's unconditional love as they walk this journey together. They are ladies of integrity, humor, spunk and class. I am honored to know them and to be called a "Spurette." They are great models of friendship and I've learned many lessons from knowing them and hearing their stories.

Jennifer Miller

A Time for a New Dream

by Karan Boyd Jamison

(daughter of Carolyn Boyd)

O my friends hear my heart; listen to the words of my mouth.
I will open my mouth in parables,
I will speak of things I want to hide, things from my past—
what I have heard and experienced, what our mothers have told us.
I will not hide them from our children;
I will tell the next generation the praiseworthy and
redeeming deeds of the Lord, his power, and the wonders he has done.
Psalm 78:1-4 (paraphrased by Karan)

*J*t is hard to even begin describing what it has meant for me to be the daughter of a SPUR. I have often thought we should be given a name equally as fitting—SPURettes, or SPURita, or perhaps even Spawn of SPUR. Yet no title seems quite expressive enough for the privilege this birthplace holds. Yet I do hold it, and hold it tightly. It has been the greatest example of commitment, of spiritual heritage, of friendship between women, and of prayer, that I have ever witnessed. These women have blessed me beyond measure. It is a most daunting task to describe my thoughts and feelings about the SPURS. You see, they are my friends, my mentors, my counselors, my roommates, my art teachers, and my mothers. It is not an editing blunder that I have capitalized "SPUR" throughout this story. To me they are an all caps group!

It was previously noted that the Spurs have been meeting for more than thirty-five years. When they meet, they pray. When they are not meeting, they pray. They pray for one another's children, spouses, and pains. I believe when you are on your knees for someone, you become invested in that person. That is exactly what they are, invested. Not only are they invested in each other, they are invested in each other's children and their children's children. They "show up" whenever the need is there. This leads me to my story.

Ever since I can remember, I always dreamed of the day I would have my own family. When I played dress up, I wanted to wear the white wedding dress and veil. I dreamed of my wedding day, the flowers I wanted, the dresses my bridesmaids would wear, how my father would walk me down the aisle, etc. My soul mate and I would gaze at each other and say the vows we had written. There would be dancing at the reception, a huge cake that we would gently shove into each other's mouths—I would be beautiful and captivating to my groom. You get the picture. Keep in mind I have been a bridesmaid fourteen times. I had plenty of experience having the showers, trying on the gowns, the dyed-to-match shoe collection and catching the bouquet. My dream grew with each wedding. Secretly, I dreamed of living my mother's life. After all, she was great, had a great husband, great kids, great friends—it was going to be GREAT!

Sounds great—Right?

I was thirty-three, a business owner, homeowner, and thought life was going well. However the desire of my heart, my dream, had not materialized. Though talks of proposals had come with different boyfriends, none felt right—like THE one. Then one day I met a man at "LUV" Airport. He was waiting for the same flight as I was. We ended up on the same flight seated next to each other. He was charming, handsome and very convincing. After a three-month whirlwind long distance courtship, we were engaged. We seemed to want the same things in life; we enjoyed the same activities, foods, and hobbies. It seemed like a perfect match. After all, we did meet at "LUV." I became so caught up in it all that I chose to be blind to the red flags. I was determined that this was the one. I needed him, and he needed me. Any problems we had could be chalked up to the fact we were apart from one another. It would all work out when we would finally be together. Plans for the wedding seemed to be coming together quite nicely—the big church, the dress, and the country club reception. It was going to be great!

My blind eye had worked pretty well during our courtship, but now there were a few red flags I could not ignore. Towards the end of our premarital counseling everything seemed to be going fine. That was until my fiancé went to the counselor for a solo visit a week before the wedding. In our next, and what was to be our last, meeting with the counselor, the counselor said he would not recommend we go through with the marriage. "WHAT?" Just last week everything was fine. What had my fiancé said to him to make him change his mind? I was spinning, trying to understand what had just happened. We were to marry the following week! Surely it was something we could work through. My fiancé was certain it was nothing he had said and the counselor was surely wrong to make such a statement. Everything would be great!

Later that week, a dear friend, one of few who would ever have enough courage, took me aside and told me she did not think our marriage was a good idea. My fiancé had not convinced her or other friends that he really loved me or deserved me. Again, "WHAT?" It was Wednesday—the wedding was scheduled for Saturday. Couldn't we have picked a better time for this conversation? Lord, what are You doing here? Don't You want me to be happy? Don't You want me to have my heart's desire?

That same evening, in a very heated and painfully destructive conversation with my fiancé, the wedding was called off. The dream had died. I went to my parents and woke them up at 1:30 a.m. on Thursday morning and told them what had happened. "The wedding is off." The three of us sat on the bed and cried. The thought of that night holds much pain in my memory of it.

The next morning, a call came from my fiancé, acting as if nothing had happened. I reminded him of our conversation the previous night and he had no recollection. He said he had taken something to help him sleep and it had put him into a hypnotic state. He wanted to fly in and come to my parents' house to see if we could mend the situation and then proceed with the wedding plans.

Then the SPURS showed up.

As you can imagine, the task of undoing what took months to pull together is daunting. We needed to call two hundred fifty of our closest friends and tell them their Saturday night was now free. No need to come to the church. There were caterers to be notified, flowers to be canceled, and gifts to be returned. The list was endless and I was in no shape to pull any of it off. Within a few days, everything had been done. Others had carried my personal shame—a perfect picture of the cross.

That was not all. That day my fiancé flew in and we all sat in my parents' living room. All of us were in tears. We tried to put some kind of order to what was such painful chaos. There came a knock at the door, and in walked Pat, a SPUR. Pat had come to stand in the gap. Not sure why she had come; God had just whispered to her she should be there—maybe to sit in the driveway and pray or be whatever assistance she could be.

As I mentioned earlier, if you had been on the heart of one of the SPURS you were on the heart of all of the SPURS, as they were invested. My fiancé had certainly made the prayer list as he and I courted. Pat knew that his parents had been deceased for some time and wanted to stand in for him as much as she wanted to be there for me. The funny thing is it gave me comfort as well. I had loved this man and he was now sitting before a broken woman and two parents who were compassionate, yet angry with the man who had broken their daughter's heart.

Pat showed up. It was obvious that the Holy Spirit nudged her to come. I know that any one of the SPURS would have wanted to be there to lend comfort that day, but Pat knew it needed to be her. Pat stayed with my fiancé and me that weekend to try to help mend two broken hearts. Even though there was a sense of numbness, her presence and counsel did bring some order and healing to a horrific time.

Some years later, I read a book that spoke of shattered dreams. I learned that God uses the pain of shattered dreams in order to help us realize our greater desire for Him and ultimately help us begin dreaming the highest of dreams. That day was just the beginning of the shattered dream. I spent the next seven years trying to make that dream, my dream, a reality. There were bad choices and wrong directions in those years that led me to the end of MY dream. My dream needed to be shattered, to die, in order to find His dream for my life.

In March 2008, I married my true soul mate. The man God had picked out for me is far better than any man I would have chosen on my own. We did gaze at each other and recite vows that we had written (from the heart, not by heart). I did not wear a beautiful white gown, nor did we have the big country club reception. There were fifty guests, not two hundred and fifty. Our attendants were our children. What Satan had sought to destroy, God redeemed for good. I no longer want to live my mother's life. Hers is still great, but I want to live mine, the one God desires for me.

Sometimes sharing our dark experiences can be painful and even shameful but I do believe it is through our experiences that God can be glorified. I think the SPURS do that in spades. Their desire is to see God glorified through their friendship, their commitment and how they love one another. The old song, "They will know we are Christians by our love" is certainly lived out in these women. I am honored by their friendship and hope I will be able to pass these same truths on to my children by "showing up" at their point of need.

A Time to Thank the Spurs

by Kristin Page-Elliott Kirkland
(daughter of Kathleen Page Clark)

Shout for joy to the LORD, all the earth.
Worship the LORD with gladness;
come before him with joyful songs. Know that the LORD is God.
It is he who made us, and we are his;
we are his people, the sheep of his pasture.
Enter his gates with thanksgiving and his courts with praise;
give thanks to him and praise his name.
For the LORD is good and his love endures forever;
his faithfulness continues through all generations.
Psalm 100:1-5

Here is how it all started:

Mom: "Won't you please reconsider writing something for our Spur book? Some of the other daughters have submitted stories. It would be so great."

Me: "Ummm—no thank you—that just isn't something I want to do. I am so busy. Next subject, please."

The other day I read a devotion that said when we are overwhelmed we just need to have faith in God to "take the next **right** step." Well, after much thought, I realized that not contributing to the book was something I would probably regret later in life. I realized this really wasn't about me. It was important to my mother, so I have decided to step outside of my "comfort zone" and give it a shot. It's a little overwhelming, but it is the **right** step to take.

So here it goes:

As I try to write something to contribute to the Spur book, I keep thinking of some "lessons" that I have learned over the years watching my mother with her dear Spur friends. Many of these lessons have actually taken me years to understand. It seems the older I get, the clearer things become. One of the many blessings of being a mother is being able to teach our children certain values. Many of these values were taught to us as children and we are just passing them on, all in different and creative ways. Our experiences in life create the timing of these lessons we give. For me, it seems a lot of them are coming later in life. As I look in the mirror and see myself "maturing," I have come to realize that my physical appearance on the outside might be looking older, but pray and believe that my spiritual inside is becoming more beautiful every day.

I am beginning to see the "big picture" of life. The other day I was talking to my daughter, Carly, about some "life issues" regarding our attitudes and choices. Being the art major I am, I always have to explain things visually. I told her that God gives us all a paintbrush, a palette and a canvas. All the different colors represent the many people and experiences in our life. It is up to us what colors we add to the painting. Like all artists, we have the ability to alter our painting. To me, this is through God's grace. If we have too much of something, we can cover it up with something better. If we don't have enough of something in our lives, we can add more. It is our picture to paint. God has given us the tools, and we have to make the choices. I pray both of my children's "paintings" are always full of color—joyful color. For myself, my painting is becoming a brighter picture every day. So much of that is attitude. I try to see the positive in everything, good or bad. For my mother, I see her painting becoming more colorful and beautiful each and every day, too.

There are so many wonderful things about the Spurs. Each woman has set an example of living a life of Faith, and for that, I am thankful. I have seen how wonderful life is with girlfriends. There is something about a bond of friendship that words can't describe. Like the Spurs, I have been so blessed with wonderful friends. I can't imagine life without them. They are always there for me. These women have comforted me on my weakest days and have celebrated with me on my greatest. We have been through all our "chapters of life" together: dating, marriage, kids, and of course, the tragic phone call when someone found their first gray hair! There have been many tears, but more than tears, there has been laughter that carries me through some of my toughest times. Very seldom does one come crying who doesn't leave laughing. Although we haven't named ourselves like you all have (that could be interesting), my friends are always there to encourage me, to guide me, or, as so well put, to "spur" me on.

So, to all the Spurs:

Thank you for always being there for my mother. Thank you for showing your children what long-lasting friendship truly is and the value it has in a person's life. Thank you for showing your daughters how important "girl-time" is. Thank you for keeping God as the center of your lives.

Thank you, Mom, for "spurring" me on so that I can contribute to the Spur book.

Blessing and Grace!

Kristin

Left to right: Son Coby, Kristin, daughter Carly and husband Kelly.
Mother's Day 2013

A Time to Dance

by Debbie Boyd Petty
(daughter of Carolyn Bergstrom Boyd)

....a time to weep and a time to laugh,
a time to mourn and a time to dance,...
Ecclesiastes 3:4

The Spurs have been a part of my life for as long as I can remember. I think the official first gathering of the Spurs was after our house burned when I was five years old. So for thirty-five years I have always known there was a 'posse' of Godly women praying me through life.

The summer before I went to college, I had the opportunity to be mentored by one of the Spurs, Sandra Talkington. We studied the virtuous woman in Proverbs and talked about who God created me to be. I still have my notes from that summer! Sandra's gentle spirit and love of the Scriptures had a big impact on me as I was leaving home and thinking about what I wanted to do with my life. It was a priority for my mom that both my sister and I have the opportunity to be mentored by women who loved Jesus and would pour themselves into us. What a great experience to have a dear friend of my mother's invest in me like that!

When I turned thirty, I went through a painful divorce. A few months after it was final, I was invited to join the Spurs on a trip to Alabama to visit Jennifer Miller, another "Spurette" (daughter of a Spur), at Camp DeSoto where she was working. Jennifer and I had become good friends our freshman year of college, and she

311

had just walked through a serious health battle. So I was eager to visit her and see how she was doing, and looking forward to just being in the presence of this loving group of women. I knew it would be good for my soul.

The most memorable night of that trip was dancing with Kathleen Elliott who had also lived through a divorce! It was a beautiful evening and we had a great dinner sitting outside and listening to music. I'm pretty sure Kathleen was the one who started the dancing—and we began to laugh and dance on the camp stage. For some reason that fun and spontaneous act left me feeling free and lighter than I had in months. I guess you could say we danced it out! I came home from that trip feeling hopeful again and positive about the future. Being in the presence of the Spurs has a way of doing that.

I think what the Spurs have is so unique and not easily replicated. They are completely committed to each other and have a level of honesty and intimacy that I have never seen anywhere else. As the daughter of a Spur, I am blessed by those relationships as well and am so thankful for their commitment to each other and to Christ.

A Time for Answered Prayer

by Lisa O'Neal Hughes
(daughter of Gayle O'Neal)

Forget the former things; do not dwell in the past.
See I am doing a new thing!
Now it springs up; do you not perceive it?
Isaiah 43:18

I guess my first memories of the Spurs would be around age twelve or thirteen. At that time, I was an unhappy, extremely confused and rebellious teenager, to say the least. I felt that life had dealt me a bad hand and my only mission was to relieve the pain. I found that relief with drugs, alcohol and people who I felt were just like me.

The lifestyle and the people I chose to be around became the beginning of a slow, painful, extremely dangerous spiral downhill for the next twenty-five years. I would describe it like a merry-go-round that was going too fast for me to jump off. I was angry with God and anyone who truly cared about me. I didn't know it at the time but I was slowly trying to kill myself and destroy any relationships that had meaning to me.

I would come and go throughout the next several years, leaving a path of destruction for the ones who loved me and dealt with me, while I would be moving on to the next phase of my hopeless existence. God and spirituality were a seed that had been embedded in me at an early age, but I was slowly killing that part of me.

During this time when I would resurface at my family's home, I would hear my mother's words "We are praying for you. These ladies love you, Lisa!" I am not even sure if I knew it was the Spurs she was talking about at the time. I was consumed with anger and resentment when I would hear my mother say, "I'm going to lunch with the ladies," while I would be headed to a filthy, cheap motel or a house that had no utilities on, full of guns, drugs, and people who had no hope. My addiction was no longer giving me a choice and I had given up on God a long time ago.

I would later find out, though, that these women had not given up on me and that their God had been carrying me when I thought I was walking through this hell all alone.

What had started out as a way to relieve my pain had now become the noose that was slowly getting tighter around my neck. Drugs, alcohol, sex, abortions, jails, hospitals and institutions were frequent and slowly extinguishing any flicker of light I had left.

Then came the next phase of my life—failed marriages and an on-again-off-again revolving door of recovery and rehabilitation versus addiction and hopelessness.

Today I am a forty-four-year-old nurse with a three-bedroom home. I am a single mom of three healthy kids, by God's grace and the prayers of these Spurs. My children are living with me. When things get crazy, I have to remind myself of one word—gratitude. My mother and these women never gave up on me nor did the God whom I so diligently tried to extinguish from my life.

If you asked me to describe my God in three words, I would have to say, "Grace, Mercy and Love."

If you asked me to describe my mother and this group of ladies who call themselves the Spurs, I would have to say, "Grace, mercy and love."

When my Mom asked me to write something about the Spurs, my words to her were "Without their prayers, I am sure I would be dead."

I can say with no doubt in my mind, I should not be sitting on my back porch right now watching my fourteen-year-old daughter plant flowers as I write this story.

I am truly grateful. I am now living out the power of prayer.

Left to right: Gayle O'Neal's daughter, Lisa Hughes, and Gayle's granddaughter, Taylor.

A Time to Pass It On
The Next Generation of Spurs
by Karan Boyd Jamison
(daughter of Carolyn Boyd)

Let it be written for a future generation,
that a people not yet created may praise the LORD:......
Psalm 102:18

By now you have read the impact the Spurs have had on one another's life and the lives of those they touch. I am privileged to know each one of these women and am inspired by their lives and their love for one another. As a daughter of a Spur, I wanted to create the same type of support for my family and myself. Yet, how do you duplicate something God has so carefully woven together? Pray for it. That is what I did.

A friend of mine who had also witnessed the deep friendship of the Spurs began to pray with me that God would do something like the Spurs in our lives, and pull in other women that would desire the same thing. Whom do you invite? How do you start? Who will come? Are we alone in this desire? How do you ask people to jump into deep water and promise them they won't be alone? To be honest, I thought it was too much to ask for and almost didn't pursue it, but God would not let that happen. He calls us to love one another, and to do it well. Psalm 37 tells us to "Commit your way to the Lord, trust in him and he will do this." So we stepped out in faith that He would do this.

Invitations went out for a luncheon. My Mother came in to talk to us about her experience with the Spurs. We asked everyone to pray about their desire to join in a group that would commit not just to pray for one another but to live life authentically together. It is not everyone's thing I know, and that is OK. Only God could knit the hearts.

The next time we met was for an overnight. I had asked those who wanted to join the group to come with a shoebox filled with things that would help illustrate their story. It could be pictures of family, tools, anything that would help visually tell her life story. I asked that everyone pick a song that connects with her. Most importantly, I asked that everyone would pray for our weekend. Pray that God would be there in ways unspeakable:

- that He would be honored by his daughters
- that Satan's attempts to keep us from it would be thwarted
- that hearts would connect
- that we would all be refreshed and encouraged
- that our families at home would be supportive and blessed by our new friendships

I never could have imagined when we asked these things that God would be there in unbelievable ways that it would literally leave me speechless. On my way there that night, God laid it on my heart that many of us hide behind a look, "our pretty," if you will. So before we began, I asked everyone to get comfy and take off all their makeup. Some were ready to kick it off, but for others, that was a significant hurdle. As always, God knew what He was doing and we began to get real very quickly. We all took turns that weekend opening our shoeboxes late into the night and the following morning—boxes of broken hearts and shattered dreams but all redeemed through Christ. We prayed for each person as she ended her story. God orchestrated every detail, even down to the order in which we spoke. Even now, as I remember that first night together, I am overwhelmed that He loves us so.

One year later we were still meeting once a month and have had other opportunities to overnight. Not everyone can come all the time, but each time, it's the right ones for the issues we are currently facing. We don't live near each other. We don't all go to the same church. Our kids vary in age. From outward appearance we are an unlikely bunch, but we are connected through Christ. I have sisters out there who know all my ugly secrets and still love me. They keep my confidences and pray with me in my struggles. I have the privilege to do the same. I love them, and pray that I love them well. We are the "Spurettes." We have a great heritage from which to learn.

Thanks Mom—and all my other mothers.

Left to right: Friends Jennifer Miller and Karan Boyd (Jamison).
Two daughters of two Spurs. 2002

A Time to be Rodeo Queens

A thank you to all the Spurs who were gathered together at Christmas 2010

by Annie Laurie Hyde
(daughter of Anne Hyde)

Every time I think of you, I give thanks to my God.
Philippians 1:3 (NLT)

*B*elow is a text message from Annie Laurie Hyde to Pat Reynolds. She sent it while we were gathered together for our 2010 Christmas gathering at Mary Jo Scheideman's lovely home. Annie Laurie was in hopes that Pat would read this to the group to express her love and gratitude to all the Spurs. We were having too much fun to hear the beep on Pat's phone, so it never got read. So Spurs, here it is:

Dear RODEO QUEENS!

Merry Christmas!
I want each of you to know from the sincere depth of my heart how much I LOVE YOU ALL!
You may not realize it, but you have been, and still are, my extended loving, understanding and compassionate family.

Thank you! Thank you for taking me in and holding me up when I couldn't walk.

It's because of EACH OF YOU and especially the love and friendship of Patricia Geis Reynolds that I feel like family.
Thank you, Spurs.
My prayer is for your continued love and "spurring."

Sometimes you need a kick to get going down the trail.
I wish you Peace and Joy down in your heart!

Merry Christmas!

Annie Laurie

P.S. Just another note:
I'm so proud of you, Molly.
I learned recently that a friend of mine is an art student of yours.
She said there is so much light around you.
You have been an inspiring teacher!
You all represent Jesus in a way I love!
OK Pat, you may read aloud.
Love you, Annie Laurie

Texted on December 10, 2010 at 1:38 p.m.

A Time to Observe
by Hannah Jones
(daughter of Elizabeth Buckley
and granddaughter of Molly Dummit)

Show me Your ways, O Lord; Teach me your paths.
Lead me in Your truth, and teach me:
For You are the God of my salvation; On You I wait all the day.
Psalm 25:4-5 (NKJV)

*O*ne of my goals in life is to seek the kind of relationships my mom (Elizabeth) and my grandmother (Molly) have with the Spurs. I have known the Spurs and watched their encouraging ways all my life. During my adolescent and stressful teen years Pat gave me wise counsel and helped me through some very rough spots. The night before my first child was born, the Spurs had a wonderful baby shower in Anne's lovely home. Kathleen even flew in from California to join in the shower. What an encouragement!

I've attended two of the Mother-Daughter Spur gatherings and have witnessed firsthand the fun and fellowship. On one special retreat, we daughters really enjoyed getting to know Georgia. Her infectious big smile was so welcoming and inclusive.

The Spurs have been a very important support system for my mom and grandmother. I have always known that they were there for me, too. Through fun and celebration, sadness and grief they have been true friends. I cherish all the memories and thank God for them.

Left to right: Three generations. Granddaughter Hannah, daughter/ Spur Elizabeth Buckley, mother/Spur Molly Dummit.

A Time of National Tragedy
Introduction by Carolyn Boyd
Letter written by Keith Boyd
(son of Carolyn Boyd)

"........Father, forgive them for, they know not what they do........"
Luke 23:34 (ESV)

Introduction

*M*y husband and I flew to Colorado Springs for a conference at Focus on the Family a few days early as we had plans to visit our friends' summer place in Cuchara, Colorado. We rented a car and arrived in Cuchara on a beautiful sunlit morning. The date was September 8, 2001.

On September 11, we were dressing for a fun day in the mountains when Jim's cell phone rang. It was our friend, Buddy Young, calling from Fort Worth who asked, "Do you have the television on?" When we replied that we didn't, he told us to turn it on as one of the twin towers in New York had just been struck by a commercial jetliner. As soon as we turned the television on, we witnessed another plane approaching the second tower.

This can't be happening—this is America—we are impervious to this kind of terror! Yet, we were seeing it with our own eyes.

We immediately tried to reach our son, Keith Boyd, who pastors Trinity Baptist Church in New York City but to no avail. Each time we dialed his number, we got busy signals. We didn't know where our New York family was as we watched the second tower go down. What a comfort it was to be with our Spur friend, Gayle O'Neal, and her husband, Richard, that day. All four of us fell to our knees and began to pray. We prayed for Keith's family. We prayed for the families who would be told of losing loved ones. We prayed for our nation as it was obviously under enemy attack. We prayed for our national leaders who would be charged with having to sort things out and comfort a nation.

Shortly after we had prayed, Jim's cell phone rang again. This time it was Keith with the comforting words that his family was safe! The following is a letter Keith wrote describing firsthand what it was like being in the City that fateful day.

Letter written by Keith Boyd, 9/14/01 after the terrorist attack on 9/11/01

I was to meet with a group of pastors Tuesday morning at the Empire State Building. I arrived a bit before nine and saw a huge cloud of smoke blowing across 5th Ave downtown in the financial district. But it wasn't rising upward as coming from a fire on the ground; it was obviously originating from somewhere up high. As I couldn't see the source from my vantage point, I asked a woman near me if she knew what was happening downtown. She told me that a plane had just crashed into one of the World Trade towers. I quickly went inside and up to my meeting on the 15th floor of the Empire. I told the people there what I had heard and we quickly found a TV. Almost immediately we saw coverage of the second plane banking into the second tower.

A couple of minutes later the emergency speakers sounded with the command to evacuate the building. The pastors I was meeting with and I left the building, went down to the corner of 5th and 34th, and began to pray. We prayed for the emergency crews that were responding. We prayed for those who were in the building, those being evacuated and those who might be trapped. We prayed for the souls of those we knew were lost and for their families.

After praying for several minutes there on the street corner we walked a couple of blocks to the office of Here's Life Inner City (a Campus Crusade ministry), located on the 17th floor. By the time we had arrived, Ted Gandy, the National Director, was looking out of the window of his conference room at the place where the south tower had been standing only moments before. Inconceivably, it was gone! So again we prayed.

There in the conference room, after several minutes of watching TV footage of the collapse, I felt the need to try to get in touch with my family. I was on the phone, trying to get a connection, standing at the window, looking south at the smoke that was coming from the barely visible edge of the north tower that was still standing (my view was partially obstructed by other buildings). All of a sudden the smoke that was smoothly streaming out of the side of the building began to churn violently and what I could see of the second tower disappeared. I turned to the TV and watched in horror as the tower totally collapsed. It was beyond comprehension. It was surreal. And so we prayed again.

In a state of shock I left Ted's office and walked from 36th Street uptown toward my apartment on E. 61st. The subway was shut down and consequently the sidewalks and streets were filled with people walking north, walking away from the southern tip of Manhattan where so much horror had occurred. And again I was struck with how surreal it all was. Normally boisterous and animated New Yorkers were walking north in an eerily somber silence. Me included.

I arrived at my apartment where I retrieved voicemail informing me that my family was okay. I was not really worried about them, as I knew they were all uptown at the time of the attack, but even so, hearing the message brought some degree of relief to my heart.

After waiting until my family was safely home and watching CNN for a couple of hours, I headed to my office at the church. We opened the doors so that people off the street could come in and pray. I went to my office, closed the door, and collapsed in my chair. I couldn't cry. I couldn't think. I couldn't even pray. All I could do was stare. I was emotionally spent. About an hour later I felt I needed to do something so I left my office and walked around the corner to the entrance of the Queensboro Bridge, one of the five bridges across the East River onto the isle of Manhattan. The police had designated one of the four sections of the bridge to foot traffic only. I stood there watching literally thousands of dazed people walking onto the bridge, leaving Manhattan to go to their homes in Queens, and almost without exception they all had a uniform blank stare, the stare that I had had for the previous hour. And upon reflection, that stare was emblematic of how thousands of New Yorkers would feel for some time to come. The stare was certainly my state of being for the next thirty hours or so.

Tuesday night we decided not to have a prayer service at the church, as getting around the city was next to impossible and I had the sense that people just wanted to go home and try to get their minds around what had transpired (as if that were possible). We did leave the church doors open, with the invitation posted outside for people to come in and pray, until about 10 p.m.. I went home about 11 p.m. emotionally and physically exhausted.

I woke up on Wednesday morning with the image of churning smoke and a disappearing building replaying in my head. As much as I tried, it was difficult to get out of bed. In truth, I'm not sure I truly wanted to get out of bed; I wasn't sure I could face what I was certain the day had in store. But by God's grace, I did get out of bed, but I went into the day still somewhat paralyzed by the stare.

We decided that we would hold a prayer service that evening and got the word out via email and phone chain, at least as much as the phone and internet connections would allow; as you might imagine, much of the city's systems had been compromised. We again opened the church doors for prayer all day. I tried to go about the business of following up on phone calls and emails and of making calls to people I knew that worked in the financial district, wondering if they had escaped the destruction. Much to my surprise, by God's grace, everyone that our staff and I could think of had gotten out physically unharmed, many with miraculous stories. And as grateful as I was to our Lord that as far as we could tell He had been merciful to our body, I still could not break out of the emotional stare that had captured me. To a significant degree I was simply going through the motions of the day.

When the prayer service started at 7:00 p.m., I wasn't any better. I kept telling myself, "Keith, you are the pastor, you are the one that people are looking to for leadership, for strength, for comfort. God is sovereign. He is good. Snap out of it." But I couldn't.

We had planned the service in the pattern of so many of the Psalms, where the psalmist begins with his honest complaint, lamenting to God the depths of his despair. As David cried out in Psalm 142:1-2:

> *".....I cry aloud to the LORD; I lift up my voice to the LORD for mercy. I pour out my complaint before him; before him I tell my trouble."*

We encouraged the people who were there (over two-hundred) that the first thing we needed to do was be honest to God with our feelings, to tell him how angry we were, how sad and frustrated and helpless; to tell him what was in the depths of our souls. And they did. And I did.

During this time I began to feel something for the first time in thirty-six hours. The stare seemed to be lifting. Something inside was being resurrected.

We then moved to a time of petition, praying for the families and friends of those missing and dead, both on the planes and in the World Trade Center and Pentagon; praying for the rescue workers and their families; praying for our government, both local and national. These petitions were heartfelt and strong. But then I instructed the congregation that Jesus calls us to pray for our enemies, so we needed to spend some time praying for those who were behind the attack and for the families of the terrorists who had lost their lives. Silence. More silence. And then a young woman in the middle of the sanctuary confessed, "Lord, I know this is what I am supposed to do, but it's so hard."

And then a man up front: "Lord, help me to forgive them even as you have forgiven me." Then someone else, and another, and another, until from every section of the sanctuary, people were praying for our enemies. We were praying protection for the Arab and Middle Eastern communities of our city, that they would not be attacked or ostracized because of hatred and racism. We were praying for the gospel of Jesus Christ to bring revival in Muslim lands. God was transforming our hearts right before my eyes.

The final season of prayer that we entered into was that of reaffirming our faith in the character of God and glorifying Him for who He is and what he would do through this event. In our planning we thought it might be difficult for the people to get to that point, but after the time of petition for our enemies, it seemed as if the people couldn't hold back their praise. A few psalms of praise were recited, a few sentence prayers affirming the sovereignty and goodness and grace of God were offered, and then a man in the back, who had earlier in the day been working with the relief effort among the rubble, spontaneously began singing, "As the deer panteth for the water so my soul longeth after thee." Chorus after chorus, hymn after hymn just began to ring out from every corner of the church. We sang a capella for over half an hour, praising the God who had saved us and who would be faithful to bring about his good purpose in the midst of this tragedy. And by the time the benediction was pronounced and the last chorus of Salvation Belongs to Our God *was sung, my soul was renewed and the stare was gone. And not just for me, but also for everyone who left that place.*

Today, Thursday, has been a day much like yesterday— phone calls and emails, tracking down people we think might have been impacted, looking into various opportunities for ministry but one thing is different. Me. The stare is gone and He who is the Life has brought renewal to mine. But even as I write I know that this ordeal is far from over, and I know the evil one will attempt to paralyze me, us, the body of Christ in this city, from doing the good works that God has prepared in advance for us to do. So pray for us. Pray that the body of Christ will know how to respond to this crisis in a way that will bring glory to God. Pray that we will somehow be a haven for those hurting. And pray for me, that I will not have a relapse of the stare and by the grace of God I will know how to lead this community of faith in a way that will be healing and representative of the goodness and grace of God.

May God be merciful.
Keith Boyd
Trinity Baptist Church, NYC

Spurred by Grace
Chapter Fifteen

Husbands of Spurs

A Time to Meet
by Hamp Miller, M.D.
(husband of Clarice Townes Miller)

*For this reason ever since I heard about your faith
in the Lord Jesus and your love for all the saints,
I have not stopped giving thanks for you,
remembering you in my prayers.*
Ephesians 1:15-16

*T*his verse, though short, represents my understanding of the Spurs. More than thirty years ago, my wife, Clarice, was invited on a surprising journey of love, prayer, support and fun. The group of women has shared their lives of wonder, happiness, sadness and everyday living. They have met in homes; traveled together throughout the U.S. and Europe. The fellowship, though great, has never eclipsed the support and sharing of happiness and sorrows.

Of course, I only observed from afar for many years, but I personally have seen the results. Clarice's highest highs, lowest lows and the in-betweens have been shared with the group. Their love, care, prayer and insight have been a blessing to her. She has received care, hope, assurance, confirmation, love, instruction and a greater knowledge of God, His Son, the Lord Jesus, and the ever-present Holy Spirit. The joy of seeing Clarice return from these gatherings refreshed and relaxed has been my gift from the Spurs.

A story that may be apocryphal is that a husband of one of the Spurs noticed that his wife was disconcerted, on edge and generally flustered. He commented to his wife, "Honey, isn't it about time for the Spurs to meet?" This is how "those on the outside" see the effects. Husbands and children get a secondary gain!

My connection with this great group of women has been through fun get-togethers. There have been organized dinners in Dallas and Fort Worth. Since our move from Denton, there have been retreats to our country home. We live fifteen miles out from Nacogdoches, Texas, on seventy acres. The Spurs have driven four or five hours from the Dallas/Fort Worth area for several retreats. During that time, these delightful ladies have blessed me. We had conversations, meals, and walks and we shared our love of Jesus. I was able to meet Spurs that I had only heard of and renewed friendships with those I had known before. Names, faces and personalities were "put together." What a wonderful gift, I too, received.

An example of primary gain I received occurred many years ago. It was the first gatherings of husbands for a dinner get-together. None of us knew quite what to expect. The ladies knew each other well but most of the husbands had never met. The ladies were asked to share something that they appreciated about their husbands. Clarice and I had just sent our oldest son off to college. A close friend of ours, a counselor, was working with a single mother with a baby. It was early winter and beginning to get very cold. The mother and child were sleeping in a car. Our friend called Clarice to ask if she knew of someone who might be able to help them. Clarice said that she thought that we could help—and so we did. The young mother and the eighteen-month-old stayed with us for four months. We kept the baby while his mother worked to save money. Clarice shared with the group how much she had appreciated my willingness to be helpful in this situation. The empty nest had been filled in a most unusual way. I shared what this had meant to me. I was able to vent my feelings about losing the special relationship with this young boy. He had helped to fill a hole in my heart. It was a tender moment for all of us. I realize that my sharing was a small portion of a fun-filled evening but my remembrance of it still lasts to this day.

Left to right: Son John Miller and father Hamp Miller

A Time of Joy Deferred
Memories of my daughter Andrea
Written by Bob Reynolds
(husband of Pat Reynolds)

...we look not at the things which are seen,
but at the things which are not seen:
for the things which are seen are temporal;
but the things which are not seen are eternal.
2 Corinthians 4:18 (KJV)

Safe in the arms of Jesus.
Inscribed on Andrea's marker at
Restland Memorial Park in Dallas, Texas.

MEMORIES
by Bob Reynolds

Andrea, Andrea.
Lovely child, dear child,
Taken from me.
Lonely child, troubled child,
Breaking toward sunshine,
Finally
Tasting life,
Promise of things to come.

Murderer! Murderer!
Taking my Andrea,
Felling her in her prime,
Shutting out the sunshine.
Hopes gone.
Space, empty space.

My daughter! My daughter!
Where have you gone?
Cut short in your youth
By a foolish man's folly.

I see your husband
But he is not there.
I see your children
But they are not there.
Hopes then,
But now what might have been.

My child! My child!
Moving from darkness to light
Before your time.

Save me a place in your new abode.
Wait for me.
Sorrow now
But joy comes.

God only will make it up to us.

©2001 Bob Reynolds

A Time to Get "Spurred"
Marriage to a Spur
by Carl Brumley
(husband of Mary Alice Brumley)

Her children arise and call her blessed;
her husband also, and he praises her:
"Many women do noble things, but you surpass them all."
Charm is deceptive, and beauty is fleeting;
but a woman who fears the LORD is to be praised.
Honor her for all that her hands have done,
and let her works bring her praise at the city gate.
Proverbs 31:28-31

*A*s I understand it, the Spurs are a group of ladies who provide concern and help for each other. They are to "spur" or encourage one another on in the good works of the Lord. These ladies, along with my wife, Mary Alice, have learned to become more concerned for others both in and out of the group. You might say this has become a goal in their lives. This group does not put thoughts of personal gain or comparison above love and friendship for each other. I like to think of them as "Spurring" each other on to become like the woman in Proverbs 31!

I went with a small number of these special ladies to Switzerland, as a preamble to the larger group traveling to Italy. We were joined by six more Spurs for a two-day trip to Venice. I was the envy of every Italian "Casanova," because I was surrounded by so many beautiful women.

Not only did I become better acquainted with these gracious ladies, I experienced the love they have for each other. The trip was educational but also very relaxing and pleasant. You might even say I was "spurred!"

Left to right: Mary Alice and Carl Brumley.

A Time for Surprises

by Tom Clark
(husband of Kathleen Page Clark)

Oh! Teach us to live well! Teach us to live wisely and well!
Surprise us with love at daybreak;
then we'll skip and dance all the day long.
Psalm 90:12,14 (The Message)

Surprise—I married a Spur!

Life is full of surprises—One surprise follows another. Surprises in my life seem interconnected.

A Life Surprise—The education, career and family choices I made throughout my life led to my marriage to Kathleen Page Clark. The same was true with the passages in Kathleen's life. Had either of us made just one different life choice, we would not have met, courted and married! We believe that our life choices were part of God's plan for us.

An Introduction Surprise—Kathleen wanted me to meet her Spur friends before our marriage. During our courtship she took me to an early morning Spurs meeting. Kathleen lovingly told me that her introduction of me to her Spurs would probably last no longer than fifteen minutes. Then it would be appropriate for me to leave their meeting. Imagine our surprise when the Spurs talked with me the entire morning! They were eager to get to know the man who had captured Kathleen's heart after she had been single for twenty-six years. They even invited me to join them for lunch! The Spurs surprised me by spilling their overflowing love for Kathleen to me.

A Communion Surprise—Months later, just before our wedding service started, the Spurs gathered with Kathleen for a time of prayer at the church. Each Spur expressed gratitude, blessings and happiness over the miracle of the moment.

Kathleen's sister, Dr. Rev. Martha Page Greene, and my brother, Canon Frank H. Clark, performed the wedding ceremony. We asked them to serve us communion as our first meal as man and wife. In turn, we served communion to our family and friends as the very first meal we offered as a married couple. That communion meal was a deeply spiritual and meaningful part of our wedding service.

I noticed during communion that the Spurs were seated in two entire rows right behind both of our immediate families. Kathleen had planned it that way, as the Spurs are a big part of her spiritual family. The majority of Spurs and their husbands came to share in our joy. Their presence was a beautiful expression of their love and support. How blessed I am to have a warm kinship with eighteen Spurs who continue to cherish the new love of my life.

A Growing Family Surprise—During the wedding service, I sat on the first seat of the first row on the right side of the aisle in the church. Seated to my right were my children and grandchildren. Across the aisle to my left were Kathleen's children and grandchildren. Both of our families were there to witness and celebrate our marriage. They were also active participants in the ceremony that united our two families.

Kathleen gained three sons, one daughter, a grandson and a granddaughter. With the simple pronouncement that we were "man and wife," I gained another son and daughter, two grandsons and four granddaughters. Kathleen and I were delighted to embrace their spouses and extended families as well. Kathleen's sisters and spouses and my siblings and spouses completed our wonderful new family. I also consider the Spurs as part of our remarkable extended family.

A Friendship Surprise—We discovered that marriage is not just a union of two people and two families. My friends became Kathleen's friends and her many friends became mine. What a wonderful wedding gift to each other!

A Homily Surprise—Kathleen's sister, Martha, said in her homily during the wedding service:

> *"You, Tom, who so faithfully attended to your wife, Pearl, at breakfast, lunch and dinner, day after day, week after week, without complaint until her death, have been given a new love and a new future. And you, Kathleen, who had resigned permanently from Match.com and eHarmony. com, had begun to believe that there was no new marriage partner for you in this life. You, who endured three total knee replacements and three inpatient physical therapy rehabilitations, found a new friend there who today is to be your husband. How good is God to give you each other, that in the autumn of life, each of you has been given someone who will hold your hand and whisper on your pillow until death do you part. What a marvelous sacred reversal to life in the midst of life. Praise be to God who turns our tears into joy, and spins all of our loose ends into a fabric of love. God's other name is 'Surprise.'"*

A Post-Wedding Surprise—Kathleen loves her new name. She discovered much to her surprise that it is not easy for a bride to change her name. The marriage license does not automatically make her name officially Clark with all the various record keepers. Her passport, Social Security card, Medicare card, insurance companies, bank accounts, credit cards, utilities, driver's license and voter registration knew her by her other married name. Changing the records was not just a matter of simply sending out notifications. Many of them required copies of the marriage certificate as proof. Kathleen had to contact each agency and business directly and in the proper order. The big surprise came as she shared her love story with each customer service representative that she was seventy and married an eighty-year-old man after twenty-six years of single life. The consistent and unexpected response to her story was always, "Oh, you give me hope!"

A New Surprise—God had even more in mind for me. He had been grooming this groom to help the Spurs publish this book of their stories for their families and for inspiration to others. Kathleen and Clarice persistently, yet patiently, encouraged the Spurs to write their stories. Getting it published was another matter and a big hurdle. God's perfect timing brought me into their ambitious project. My interest in website programming, design and layout seemed to be the skills the Spurs needed. It was a natural transition for me to help prepare their book for self-publishing with Xulon Press. That is how their dream finally became a reality and an answer to prayer.

I wonder what surprise God has planned for me—and for you—next?

Left to right: Kathleen and Tom Clark on their wedding day.
May 27, 2012.

Epilogue
by Harriet Wallace

O God, you have taught me from my earliest childhood,
and I constantly tell others about the wonderful things you do,
Now that I am old and gray, do not abandon me, O God.
Let me proclaim your power to this new generation,
your mighty miracles to all who come after me.
Psalm 71:17-18 (NLT)

*T*his is not the end of the Spurs' stories. The book of our life as individuals and as a group continues. Jesus Christ is the author and we are just walking through the pages. We have invited you into a few chapters of our book to give glory to the One who gives us life and to encourage you to keep trusting in your Heavenly Father who always wants to do the most loving thing for you.

You have stories. Write them. They will live on long after you walk through the last pages of your book.

Spur Bios

"The Lᴏʀᴅ bless you and keep you;
The Lᴏʀᴅ make His face shine upon you,
And be gracious to you;
The Lᴏʀᴅ lift up His countenance upon you,
And give you peace."
Numbers 6:24-26 (NKJV)

*E*ach Spur has made an impact on her family, church community, state, nation and world with her volunteer activities. The areas of volunteer work vary and include teaching, fund raising, board members, committee members, retreat speakers, mentoring, and mission work locally and globally. On these short bios, we have not listed these individually. Each Spur uses her God-given talent to be glory reflectors. Under the chapter titled "A Time to Serve," we have anonymously listed these areas of ministry to show the commitment and the involvement of the Spurs. To God be the glory!

Carolyn Bergstrom Boyd was born in Austin, Texas, from a long line of Texas Bergstroms (hence the Austin Bergstrom International Airport). She has three children and seven grandchildren. Carolyn stays busy being her husband's right hand as he ministers to the senior adults in their church. Carolyn is the one who called the first Spur meeting over thirty-five years ago. Her daughter Karan has started a Spur group of younger gals in San Antonio. Carolyn job-shared with Sandra, another Spur, as a purchasing assistant at American Airlines and has since retired. Carolyn has two life verses. The first one is Psalm 138:8: *The Lord will fulfill his purpose for me; your love, O LORD, endures forever—do not abandon the works of your hands.* The second one is Isaiah 43:1b: *Fear not, for I have redeemed you; I have summoned you by name; you are mine.*

Mary Alice Cowen Brumley was born in Shawnee, Oklahoma. She has a Bachelor of Science degree from the University of Oklahoma. She and her husband have six children and seventeen grandchildren. Mary Alice has always been very active in church, community, civic and service organizations. She is retired from American Airlines. Her life verse is John 8:32 (NASB): *....and you will know the truth, and the truth will make you free.*

J. Elizabeth Davis Buckley was born in Valparaiso, Florida, and currently lives in Lexington, Kentucky. Elizabeth is our only daughter of a Spur, Molly Dummit, who has been a Spur since their first retreat over thirty-five years ago. Elizabeth has seven children and nine grandchildren. Elizabeth's formal training is as a registered nurse. Art, however, has been a passion and natural expression all of Elizabeth's life. She has very little formal training but a rich genetic heritage through her mother, Molly. Elizabeth does murals as well as portraits and landscapes using all kinds of media. You can see her art at the following website: http://ebuckley.com. Elizabeth's life verse is Ephesians 1:17-21 (NKJ): *....that the God of our Lord Jesus Christ, the Father of glory, may give to you the spirit of wisdom and revelation in the knowledge of Him, the eyes of your understanding being enlightened; that you may know what is the hope of His calling, what are the riches of the glory of His inheritance in the saints, and what is the exceeding greatness of His power toward us who believe, according to the working of His mighty power which He worked in Christ when He raised Him from the dead and seated Him at His right hand in the heavenly places, far above all principality and power and might and dominion, and every name that is named, not only in this age but also in that which is to come.*

Kathleen Page (Elliott) Clark was born in Berkeley, California and has lived most of her adult life in Texas. She attended Stanford University earning a degree in Education. Kathleen taught elementary school for a few years and then went to work for American Airlines for twenty-two years as a Passenger Service Agent. Kathleen was single for twenty-six of her years as a Spur and is known to many as Kathleen Page Elliott. Since her recent marriage, she has proudly acquired a new name, Kathleen Page Clark, and now has six children and eight grandchildren. Kathleen has two life verses: *Be joyful always: pray continually; give thanks in all circumstances, for this is God's will for you in Christ Jesus.* (1Thessalonians 5:16) and *But the fruit of the Spirit is love, joy, peace, patience, kindness, goodness, faithfulness, gentleness and self-control....* (Galatians 5:22-23).

Barbara J. Clarkin was born in Chicago, Illinois, grew up in Columbus, Ohio, lived in several different states while her husband was in the service and moved to Fort Worth, Texas, in 1965. She has seven children, one deceased, thirty-seven grandchildren and twelve great-grandchildren who keep her very busy and happy. Barbara has a B.S. in nursing from Ohio State University, working only a few years before becoming a mother, homemaker and almost full-time volunteer. She has been involved in various children, community and church endeavors while giving a helping hand to many friends. In her various activities her role was most often as "Chief" but she now prefers the part of "Indian." Her favorite life verse is Isaiah 40:31: *... but those who hope in the LORD will renew their strength. They will soar on wings*

like eagles: they will run and not grow weary, they will walk and not be faint.

Molly Dummit was born in Montgomery, Alabama. She has lived most of her life in Fort Worth, Texas. Molly has four children, nine grandchildren and eleven great-grand-children. Molly attended New Orleans Baptist Theological Seminary and the University of South Florida, studying child-hood education at both places. She has attended many art education courses and workshops and is a very respected artist. Molly taught in a private elementary school for three years. She currently teaches private and group art classes in her home. Her life verse is Colossians 4:2 (NKJV): *Set your mind on things above, not on things on the earth.*

Lois Maureen Kelsey Eagan was born in Chicago, Illinois, and lived there until she was six years old. During her public school years, she lived in Atlanta, Georgia, moved to New Orleans, Louisiana, Oberlin, Ohio and Dallas, Texas. She attended Stephens College for women in Columbia, Missouri, with a major in Fashion Design and a Minor in art and jour-nalism. Maureen has a daughter and a deceased son. She has five grandchildren (one is deceased) and five great-grandchildren. Maureen became a Christian in 1959 while watching a Billy Graham crusade on televi-sion. Maureen has had varied work experiences: a sketch artist for a clothing designer, a receptionist at a Dallas law firm, and a lover and dealer of antiques. After her husband's death, she did Junior League shows and antique shows for ten years. Her life verse is: 2 Corinthians 3:17-18: *Now the Lord is the Spirit, and where the Spirit*

of the Lord is, there is freedom. And we, who with unveiled faces all reflect the Lord's glory, are being transformed into his likeness with ever-increasing glory, which comes from the Lord, who is the Spirit.

Anne Johnson Hyde was born in Fort Worth, Texas. She attended Texas Christian University and the University of Texas. She has three children and seven grandchildren. Anne has worked as a legal secretary. Her life verse is Matthew 19:26: *With man this is impossible, but with God all things are possible.*

Carolee (Mimi) Taylor Mack was born in Phoenix, Arizona. She attended the University of Arizona receiving a B.A. in Education. She also attended the Arizona State University graduate school. Mimi has been a teacher for non-English speaking children. Mimi has three children, six grandchildren and one great-grandchild. Her life verse is Psalm 18:32-34: *It is God who arms me with strength and makes my way perfect. He makes my feet like the feet of a deer; he enables me to stand on the heights. He trains my hands for battle; my arms can bend a bow of bronze.*

Clarice Townes Miller was born in Grenada, Mississippi. She attended Belhaven College in Jackson, Mississippi, acquiring a degree in Education. She worked on a Masters in Child Development at Texas Women's University. She is the mother of four children and nine grandchildren. She has lived in a variety of places but her Mississippi accent has never left her. She has spent most of her adult life in Denton and Nacogdoches, Texas. Clarice taught third grade at Juliette Low Elementary in Savannah, Georgia. Like all the Spurs, she has spent most of her adult life doing lots of volunteer work in the church, schools and community. Clarice has two life verses. The first is: Hebrews 11:1: *Now faith is being sure of what we hope for and certain of what we do not see.* The second one is Romans 8:38-39: *For I am convinced that neither death nor life, neither angels nor demons, neither the present nor the future, nor any powers, neither height nor depth, nor anything else in all creation, will be able to separate us from the love of God that is in Christ Jesus our Lord.*

Gayle Scott O'Neal was born in Lamar County, Texas, (Direct, Texas). Gayle has lived in Texas most of her life. She has four children and thirteen grandchildren. Gayle attended Texas Christian University and graduated with a degree in Education and Speech Pathology. She taught the deaf at the Pilot School for the Deaf in Dallas, Texas. A highlight was to spend a day with Helen Keller. Gayle's passion is teaching the Bible. She was the teaching leader for BSF (Bible Study Fellowship) for twenty years in Fort Worth, Texas. Her life verse is: Proverbs 3:5-6 (NKJV): *Trust in the LORD with all your heart, and lean not*

on your own understanding; In all your ways acknowledge Him, And He shall direct your paths.

Sally Tull Renshaw was born in Plain-view, Texas. She attended Texas Christian University. Sally has four children, nine grandchildren and five great-grandchildren. She worked in a pharmacology lab. Her favorite scripture is Philippians 4: 6-7: *Do not be anxious about anything, but in everything, by prayer and petition, with thanksgiving, present your requests to God. And the peace of God, which transcends all understanding, will guard your hearts and your minds in Christ Jesus.*

Pat Geis Reynolds was born in Hobbs, New Mexico. She is the mother of three, grandmother of two and great-grandmother of five. Pat has spent most of her life in Texas. She has degrees in counseling and social work from University of Arkansas, North Texas State University and Michigan State University. Pat is a certified teacher and taught emotionally disturbed children. She is a licensed counselor and has a private practice in Dallas, Texas. She has been the director of Restoration Center in a church, a family counselor at the Callier Clinic, a coordinator for the Mental Retardation for the State of Texas, a social worker for Hope Cottage Adoption agency and a clinical social worker for a Michigan Psychiatric Outpatient Clinic. Pat's personal life verse is Philippians 3:10: *I want to know Christ and the power of his resurrection and the fellowship of sharing in his suffering.* Pat's career life verse is Isaiah 61:1: *The Spirit of the Sovereign LORD is on me, because the LORD has anointed me to*

preach good news to the poor. He has sent me to bind up the bro-
kenhearted, to proclaim freedom for the captives and release from
darkness for the prisoners.

Sandra Marie Adams Talkington was born in Ackerly, Texas. She has lived most of her life in Arlington, Texas. Sandra attended Texas Tech University and Southern Methodist University. She has a B.A. in Elementary Education. She has three sons and three grandchildren. Sandra has taught second grade, was a secretary for Manpower, and retired from American Airlines as a purchasing assistant. Sandra's life scripture is Philippians 4:4-8 (NASB): *Rejoice in the Lord always. I will say it again: Rejoice! Let your gentleness be evident to all. The Lord is near. Do not be anxious about anything, but in every-thing, by prayer and petition, with thanksgiving, present your requests to God. And the peace of God, which transcends all under-standing, will guard your hearts and your minds in Christ Jesus. Finally, brothers, whatever is true, whatever is noble, whatever is right, whatever is pure, whatever is lovely, whatever is admirable— if anything is excellent or praiseworthy—think about such things.*

Harriet Jane Wallace was born in Apollo, Pennsylvania. She currently lives in Dallas, Texas. Harriet has two children and six grandchildren. She attended Texas A&M University. Harriet is a retired school coun-selor and a Licensed Professional Counselor. Her life verse is John 3:16 (KJV): *For God so loved the world, that he gave his only begotten Son, that whosoever believeth in him should not perish, but have everlasting life.*

Phyllis Webster White was born in Jacksonville, Illinois. Her family moved to Fort Worth, Texas, when she was fourteen. Phyllis attended Texas Christian University. She has three children, five grandchildren and one great-grandchild. Phyllis owned and operated a clothing store for thirty-six years. The Clothes Horse grew into a successful lady's designer apparel store in Fort Worth. She credits God for the huge success of her business. Phyllis has two favorite scriptures: John 3:16: *For God so loved the world that he gave his one and only Son, that whoever believes in him shall not perish but have eternal life* and Lamentations 3:22-23 (RSV): *The steadfast love of the LORD never ceases, his mercies never come to an end; they are new every morning; great is thy faithfulness.*

Carol Kinney Williams was born in Dallas, Texas. At age six, polio paralyzed her from the neck down but with an unyielding spirit and determination she has had an amazing life. She has three children and four grandsons. She loves playing the piano, especially to accompany her husband, Jimmy, to sing. They are both outstanding musicians. She has travelled the world in a wheelchair. Her passion in life is to share the love of Christ with total strangers—in a taxi, airplane or grocery store! Often her opening question is, "What do you think about God?" She has a zest and love of life and others that is contagious. Her life verse is Isaiah 41:9-10: ....'*You are my servant!' For I have chosen you and will not throw you away. Don't be afraid, for I am with you. Don't be discouraged, for I am your God. I will strengthen you and help you. I will hold you up with my victorious right hand.*

Memorials
Remembering our Spur family

*Precious in the sight of the L*ORD
is the death of his saints.
Psalm 116:15

Spurs

Janet Sheats
8/2/1939 – 1/10/2007

Carolyn Driggers Mallone
5/26/1939 – 8/9/2008

Suzanne (Suzie) Murray
1/18/1937 – 12/31/2009

Georgia Smith
2/23/1928 – 11/27/2010

Mary Jo Scheideman
4/13/1931 – 10/2/2012

Husbands of Spurs

Hugh Driggers
2/26/1937 – 3/13/1987

Woody Eagan
10/11/1924 – 2/3/1992

Garland Dummit
3/3/1929 – 12/21/1993

George Mallone
11/28/1944 – 8/23/1995

Richard Hyde
6/30/1932 – 9/28/2011

Children of Spurs

Andrea Reynolds
1/23/1971 – 7/12/1991

Jeff Davis
7/12/1947 – 12/5/2006

Bo Driggers
3/29/1959 – 4/10/1996
NO PHOTO
AVAILABLE

Rex Eagan
5/26/1954 – 10/24/2008

Kevin Scott Capper
9/29/1957 – 3/17/2009

Grandchildren of Spurs

Zach Eagan

3/15/1992 — 7/6/2010

For further information, please visit us at:
www.SpurredByGrace.com

CPSIA information can be obtained at www.ICGtesting.com
Printed in the USA
LVOW08s0702210713

343782LV00003B/5/P